# PHOTO-IMAGING
## *for Painters*

### An Artist's Guide to Photoshop®
### & Elements®

**By Johnnie Liliedahl**

*Graphic layout by Heather Lim*

# Photo-Imaging for Painters

## An Artist's Guide to Photoshop® and Elements®

by Johnnie Liliedahl

Copyright 2005 by Johnnie Liliedahl, All Rights Reserved
Printed in the U.S.A.

Publisher
Liliedahl Publications
div. of Liliedahl Enterprises, Inc.
808 S. Broadway St.
La Porte TX 77571-5324
www.lilipubs.com

ISBN 0-9770734-0-8

*For Ralph*

*whose infinite patience and encouragement
allowed me to discover a whole new visual world*

Johnnie Liliedahl

# $\mathscr{A}$cknowledgements

This book is the result of my partner's unfailing belief that technology can make one's life and work, easier and more creative. My husband, Ralph, introduced me to the world of computers in the mid-eighties, when I thought I could not possibly ever need anything other than a typewriter for my work as an artist.

Imaging programs were not available for mere mortals (or starving artists) at that time, but he foresaw that new computer programs and better hardware were about to explode on the market for the casual and home user. He steadily plied me with desktop publishing programs that could do increasingly marvelous things, and soon I found myself self-publishing art instruction booklets, books, etc., and creating a small business for myself.

We were among the first users of many software-imaging programs. Ralph would test new ones before showing me their useful features. We went through many programs that were great (at the time), eventually to be replaced by ever-more-powerful ones. My first use of Adobe Photoshop® was to resize and print photographs of my paintings to illustrate art instruction books I was writing. Photoshop® allowed me to publish my painting instruction lessons in fully illustrated formats, since I could manipulate my photographs without having to go through a third party, a professional photo lab.

I soon learned that I could manipulate images for other reasons, such as making preparatory studies before beginning a painting. This book is the result of years of searching through Photoshop® for the features that can enhance and translate my reference photographs into usable images for painting, and to use photos of my completed paintings in new and different ways. I've bought countless books on the uses of Photoshop®, but none seemed directed at the needs of a painter. Most of the tutorials seemed directed at other users, because they didn't show me how I could use the features to help me paint paintings.

Without the constant encouragement, assistance and help in digging out information in the Photoshop® Help files from Ralph, I could not have learned as much as I have. This book is the result of his persistence in helping me overcome the frustration I experienced in learning some of the simplest tools that Photoshop® has to offer, and to him I am eternally grateful.

Also, a special thanks goes to Heather Lim, who was invaluable as my assistant, layout artist, proofreader and tester for all the exercises contained in this tutorial, as well as our Mac resource.

*Liliedahl*

# $\mathcal{T}$able of Contents

- *Toolbox*
- *Menu & Tool Options Bar*
- *Window Menu*
- *Zoom Tool & View Options*
- *Correcting Mistakes - Undo/Redo*
- *History Palette*
- *Layers Palette*

*Detail from "Country Girl"*
*Original Oil Painting by Johnnie Liliedahl*

# $\mathcal{E}$xercises

# $\mathcal{I}$NTRODUCTION

With the advent of the computer and the digital camera, artists now have more flexibility and options than ever before for designing paintings from their photographic resources.

This tutorial is not a substitute for painting and drawing on location, or working with the live model or the still life setup. It is presumed that the reader already knows how to paint from life, or is pursuing education in that discipline. Without this knowledge, it would be difficult to fully realize the potential that your computer and photographs can offer as painting aids.

You will always have to make artistic judgements about the color and value relationships that you wish to portray in paintings, regardless of the references you use. What you can do is explore more possibilities than ever before for ideas and compositions in your paintings with the help and aid of the computer.

Photoshop® is a powerful image-manipulation program, but the best results are always dependent on how good your initial photograph is. Before presuming that just any photograph is suitable for a painting reference (and manipulation in Photoshop®), you should know a few basics about how to select or take good photographs.

## FILM CAMERAS AND SCANNERS

Most painters like myself have literally hundreds (or thousands) of photographs we have collected through the years to use as painting references. We can now make use of them easily by importing them into Photoshop® as a digital file and resize, crop, enlarge, or change the color as we wish—a set of choices that simply didn't exist for us just a few short years ago. Unless, of course, you had access to a professional photo lab, and very deep pockets to pay for 16x20 enlargements of your thousands of photos!

To convert your film photos into digital images (so they can be used in Photoshop®), you will need a scanner, or a friend who has one and will let you use it. There are a few things you need to remember when scanning photos for use in your computer.

- If you intend to print out the images at full canvas size (i.e., 16x20, etc.), you need to scan your 4x6 photographs at a high resolution (at least 300 pixels per inch). If you scan at a lower resolution, you will not be able to blow up the small photograph to a larger print size and maintain the photo's clarity and detail.

- High resolution images require a lot of memory on your computer's hard drive. If you have severely limited space on your hard drive, you should store your large images on CD's and only keep one image saved on your computer at a time. It is also a good idea to keep images backed up on CD's anyway, for safe keeping. Keeping only one large image stored on your computer at a time will preserve the speed of the working memory in your computer.

- Scan and enlarge your photograph simultaneously by selecting an "output" size larger than your 4x6 photo. The size of your image will be limited only by your storage capacity. I don't recommend scanning an image in sizes larger than 8x10 at 300 ppi, unless you have virtually unlimited storage. Images larger than this can slow down your computer's speed significantly, even if you have a very fast, new computer.

Scanners offer a wide range of options for correcting color cast, contrast, size, etc., and you should take advantage of those features that will give you the best results. The scanner is a necessary intermediary tool to convert your film photos to digital files.

Alternatively, you may send your photos or negatives to a lab that can scan and convert your photos to digital files and provide them back to you on CD. If you choose this avenue, be certain that the files you get back are high resolution images with at least 300 ppi. Lower resolutions are a waste of time (and money) for the procedures you are about to learn.

# DIGITAL CAMERAS

The easiest photographs to use are those which are already in digital format, namely those we take by the hundreds with our new digital cameras. With the choice of high, medium, and low resolutions on each camera, which corresponds to the number of images each memory card can hold, we frequently opt for the lowest resolution so that we can take a maximum of photographs on a single card.

The problem with this choice is that we get the poorest images possible for use in Photoshop®. While I know it is boring to read the manual that comes with your digital camera, there are a few things you should absolutely learn about taking photos with them:

- **Always choose the highest resolution possible**, usually defined as "High" or "Fine". Unless you are preparing your images for giclee or off-set printing, you do not have to use the "Camera Raw" image resolution. Only the newest digital cameras give you this option, but it allows you to capture as much information as a film camera image. Beware of file sizes with Camera Raw images, however, as they are excessively large.

- **Get a tripod and a shutter release cable** for your camera, and turn off the automatic flash permanently. If you are taking photographs indoors with a lighting setup on your model or still life, a flash will destroy the composition of light and shadows. This is the single most important thing you can do to improve your photographs taken for painting reference.

- **Learn how to use the White Balance feature** on your camera. This feature determines the color of the light illuminating your subject and will assure the photograph shows the true colors, eliminating the yellow or green tinge seen in many film camera photographs. Film cameras require that you choose the right film for the type of light source you are using to get natural color. If you move from outdoors to indoors, you have to change the type of film in a traditional camera to compensate for the difference in the color of the light. With the digital camera, all you have to do is reset the white balance, a great convenience over film cameras.

- **Learn to "bracket" your exposures** by taking three photos of each setup; one at normal setting, one at +1 f-stop overexposed, and at -1 f-stop underexposed. This is a good practice for film cameras as well. Overexposing a photo will allow you to see the details in the shadow areas, but you will sacrifice the details in the lighter areas. Underexposing a photo will let you see all the detail in the lightest areas, but the dark areas will appear black. Normal settings let you see everything in between with great detail, but you may not see the lightest lights or darkest darks. In Photoshop®, you can merge the three photos and take the parts each exposure has to offer.

No camera (film or digital) can ever see all the fine gradations that the human eye can see. The reason is that the aperture setting (opening in the lens) is a fixed size, determined either by an automatic sensor, or a manual setting by the photographer. Whichever method is used to set the aperture, the camera sees only with its single, fixed "eye."

The human eye, on the other hand, constantly responds to changes in light and dark by automatic reflexes in the pupil. When we look into a brightly lit area, the pupil constricts without our even being aware of it. This allows us to see detail in very light areas. The flip side of this reflex is that when we look into darker areas, our pupils dilate to admit more light. And, as a result, we can see details in dark areas very clearly. Again, this happens so quickly, by reflex, that we are unaware of the change in our pupils.

The camera can see clearly ONLY in one area or the other, not both simultaneously. This is the most important disadvantage in using photographs as painting references. You can never get all the information you need from a single photograph; that is, until the advent of computer-enhanced imaging.

## GETTING STARTED WITH THIS TUTORIAL

We will be using the Adobe® Photoshop® program to manipulate the images found on the companion CD's for this tutorial. All the changes we will make to the photographs will be demonstrations of the types of image preparations that are ideal for creating painting resources. Rarely is an unaltered photograph alone perfect for this purpose. With Photoshop®, we will be able to enhance, change, or combine elements in photographs to provide more detail and accuracy in our references. Not only will we be enhancing existing photos, but we will also be creating entirely new compositions from multiple photos.

Careful planning of a painting composition can save enormous amounts of time once the painting process has begun. A well planned painting has less chance of becoming overworked with mistakes and revisions. Once the tools in Photoshop® are understood, photo enhancements and compositional studies can be created in a fraction of the time that it would take to do them through drawing and painting alone.

**Copy Images to Hard Drive**

 **IMPORTANT~**

**Copy the folder called Photo-Imaging Pics from the CD labeled Disc One to your hard drive before beginning the exercises. This folder contains the images that you will be opening and using for the exercises. You may choose to put this folder on drive C: on your computer, or other drive that has the most free space available.**

Copying the Photo-Imaging Pics folder to your computer will assure that you can perform the exercises at the highest speed your computer will allow. It will also allow you to preserve the original images on the CD, and retrieve a pristine copy, should you irreversibly damage an image during the exercise process, or wish to repeat the tutorial at some time in the future. The images from the Next Step Images folder on Disc Two may be copied to your hard drive as needed, but do not have to be copied in the first stages.

**<u>Save all your work to the Photo-Imaging Pics folder on your computer</u>** as you perform the exercises. It is recommended that you work entirely from this folder on your computer since you cannot save files to the CD. We will be changing files, creating new files, and opening them again later from this folder so it will be important to keep your files organized where you can find them again. It is also helpful to stay consistent with the file names that are given in the exercises because some of them will need to be identified when they are called for later in the tutorial.

## Saving Tutorial Files Under New Names

When a file must be saved with new name, go to **File** under the top menu and choose **Save As**. Choose the Photo-Imaging Pics folder, type in the suggested file name with a .tif or .psd extension (depending on instruction), press OK. If you are saving the file with a .tif extension the TIFF options window will then appear. Just press OK; take no action.

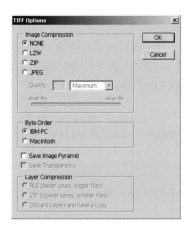

*Tiff Options window appears when saving .tif files. Just press OK.*

**Next Step Images, Skipping Exercises or Steps -** If you want to save time or skip a step in one of the longer exercises in this tutorial, you can choose a **Next Step Image** from the Next Step Images folder on Disc Two. There you will find files from many of these exercises at intermediate and finished stages. Notifications of specific Next Step Image files that are available on your Disc Two CD will appear in blue at appropriate times throughout the tutorial. Disc Two may also come in handy if you decide you would like to see what some of the later exercise steps look like when they are complete, before you finish them yourself.

## Using PC & Mac Computers

The exercises in this tutorial may be performed on either the PC or the Mac. Always use the left button on your mouse to perform these exercises. If you have a Mac, the mouse may only have one button and this will work fine. Some of these exercises can be performed by the use of (mostly optional) key command shortcuts that are given in parenthesis. The key command shortcuts are given for the PC but are very similar to Mac shortcuts. The main difference usually for Mac Computers is that the Ctrl (Control) key on the PC is replaced by the Command key on the Mac. The Alt key on the PC is most often replaced by the Option key on the Mac. The Command and Option keys are located in the same respective places as the Ctrl and Alt keys on the PC. Whenever the Enter key is mentioned, this refers to the Return key, if you have this instead on your keyboard.

## The Purpose of this Tutorial

Photoshop® is a powerful, full-featured, software program that allows you to reach a specific result by many routes. There are countless ways to make the same correction to, or manipulation of, an image. This tutorial does not purport to show you all of these features. There are countless "bibles" and encyclopedic tomes on the market that do this very well. I suspect if you had wanted to go that route, you wouldn't have purchased this very specialized tutorial.

I have included in this edition only those tools that have made my photographs more useful as painting resources. For Photoshop® (or any other imaging software) to serve the painter, it must first be understood what a painter looks for. This requires knowledge of basic painting principles and concepts. Neither this book, nor Photoshop®, will teach you how to paint. That must come from a different source.

However, armed with knowledge about how to paint, you can mine your photo references more profitably if you know your way around Photoshop®.

**Photoshop® Elements®** ~ Many casual users of photo-imaging programs opt to purchase the "lite" version of Photoshop®, marketed as Photoshop® Elements®. Almost all of the exercises in this tutorial can be performed in Elements® using the same tools contained in Photoshop®. The menu structure in Elements® is slightly different, and many of the Photoshop® functions are located in other places in Elements®, although they behave exactly the same.

To assist those users of Elements®, we have included a short note at the end of each exercise, noting where the user can find the same or similar features in their program to perform the exercises. All of the illustrations of the screen shots in this tutorial are taken from the full-featured program, Photoshop® 7.0 or Photoshop® CS. Most screens in Elements® are similar, but they may differ in size and shape. Sometimes, the titles of the screens are slightly different, and the notes contained in the purple boxes contain important information about these variations. All content that is specific to Elements® will be contained in text boxes of this color at the end of each exercise, and you should read those before you attempt any of the exercises.

As the author of this tutorial, I admit that I do not use Elements®, but I was able to find every available function that correlates to those in Photoshop® by browsing the Help (Glossary) in Elements®. There are a few advanced functions explored in this tutorial that are presently beyond the capability of Elements®. You may be the judge of how often you will need to use these functions, only available in Photoshop®. As Elements® is improved and more features added, it may not be long before it is as full-featured as Photoshop®, for the uses we need as painters.

## NAVIGATING PHOTOSHOP®

As this book is being written, the latest version of Photoshop® is Photoshop® CS. With each new edition of the software, some of the menus change, new features are offered, or may be located in a different place than in a previous version.

I have attempted to show as many features as I currently use on both Version 7.0 and Version CS, and you should know that the illustrations seen in the Exercises may vary slightly from the look on your screen if you are using versions of Photoshop® that are earlier than 7.0. Some features demonstrated in these exercises are available only on 7.0 and CS, or are located in an entirely different place on your screen. For example, the Extract command is now located under the Filters menu on CS, but was previously located under the Image, Adjustments menus on Version 6.0. The Color Match command is available only on CS.

If you are using Versions 4.0, 5.0, or 6.0, and you cannot find the menus mentioned in this tutorial (for 7.0 and CS), go to your Help menu and search for the term used in the tutorial in the Index, and it will direct you to the proper menu in your version. If the function does not exist in the earlier versions, you will not find it listed in the Help Index, and should upgrade your software to be able to use the new tools.

Before we begin the exercises, you should be familiar with several key functions that we will be using the most. In this tutorial, we will often refer to the tools and menu items found in the Toolbox, Tool Options bar, Menu bar and Window menu of Photoshop®. It is also helpful to know how to recover from a mistake, and that you can recover by several methods. And lastly, a short introduction to one of the most powerful tools in Photoshop®, the Layers palette, will give you a tour around this window to learn its terminology and iconography.

## Toolbox

The Toolbox is normally on the left side of your screen but can be moved by clicking on the blue title bar at the top of it, holding your mouse button down, and dragging it to another place on your screen. Please take a moment to familiarize yourself with the Toolbox on your computer by clicking on each tool choice. Notice that when you select each new tool in the Toolbox, different options appear on the Tool Options bar at the top of the screen. It is important to make sure that you have the correct tool selected in the Toolbox when you begin to work on your photo in Photoshop®. A small triangle in the lower right of the tool icon means that there are hidden tools. Holding the mouse button down over this tool will reveal the hidden tools.

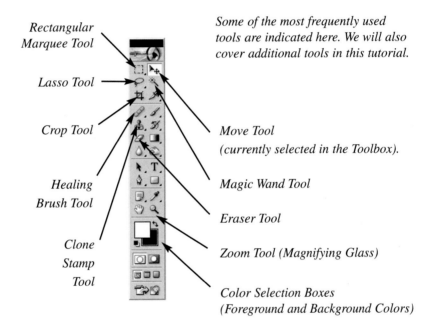

*Rectangular Marquee Tool*

*Lasso Tool*

*Crop Tool*

*Healing Brush Tool*

*Clone Stamp Tool*

*Some of the most frequently used tools are indicated here. We will also cover additional tools in this tutorial.*

*Move Tool (currently selected in the Toolbox).*

*Magic Wand Tool*

*Eraser Tool*

*Zoom Tool (Magnifying Glass)*

*Color Selection Boxes (Foreground and Background Colors)*

**Elements®** ~ The Elements® Toolbox is arranged slightly differently than this, but all the tools referenced above are available in Elements®.

## Menu & Tool Options Bar

Look at the Menu and Options bar which is located at the very top of your screen when the program is open.

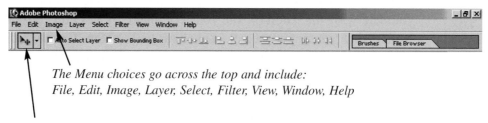

*The Menu choices go across the top and include:*
*File, Edit, Image, Layer, Select, Filter, View, Window, Help*

*The Options bar below the Menu has the Move Tool indicated because it is selected*
*in the Toolbox already shown. (This is a shortened view of the Menu and Options bar*
*in Photoshop® 7.0.)*

The Options bar can be moved by clicking on the left side of it and dragging it with the mouse. For these exercises we will leave the Options bar at the top of the screen, its default position.

***Menu and the Options bar with Options bar removed from the Menu***

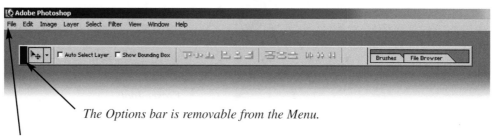

*The Options bar is removable from the Menu.*

*The Menu bar cannot be moved.*

Various options appear in the Options bar depending on the Toolbox item selected. A picture of the tool selected will appear on the left side of the Options bar. Some tool options in the Options bar have numerical settings that can be changed and entered.

Notice also the drop down menus that appear when you click on each one of the Menu options. Some of the listed menu items may be "grayed out" because they are not currently available. This may be because those options don't apply to what you are working on, or because the corresponding tool in the Toolbox has not been selected. The black triangle next to some of the menu items means that there are further drop-down menu choices. A check mark next to any item in the View or Window menus means that it is already activated. If you select (or click on) an item that is already checked, it will become unchecked and deactivated.

## Window Menu

In these exercises we will be accessing various Windows or palettes. If you cannot find one of these on your screen, it is probably not activated in the Window drop down Menu at the top. If it is activated, it will have a check mark next to it. To activate or deactivate one of the Windows or palettes here, drag your pointer over an item and release the mouse button. The window or palette will then appear or disappear on your screen.

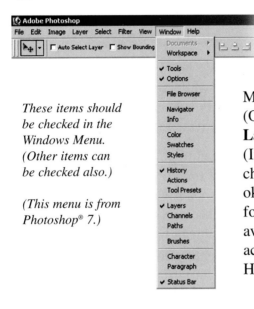

*These items should be checked in the Windows Menu. (Other items can be checked also.)*

*(This menu is from Photoshop® 7.)*

Make sure that **Tools** (Toolbox), **Options** (Option bar), **History** (History palette), **Layers** (Layer palette), and **Status Bar** (Information bar at the bottom) are checked. If others are also checked that is okay, but these palettes are what we will focus on. The Actions palette will be available on the History palette (when it is activated) through the tab at the top of the History palette window.

## Zoom Tool & View Options

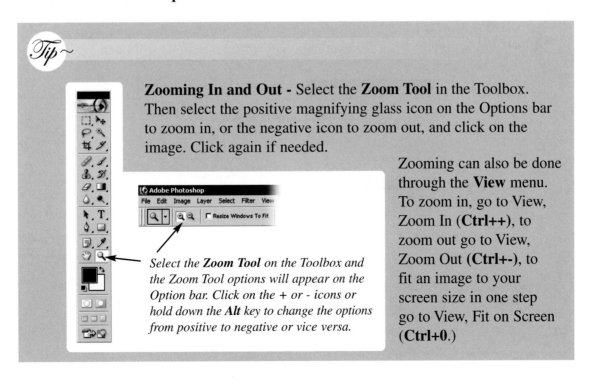

**Zooming In and Out -** Select the **Zoom Tool** in the Toolbox. Then select the positive magnifying glass icon on the Options bar to zoom in, or the negative icon to zoom out, and click on the image. Click again if needed.

*Select the **Zoom Tool** on the Toolbox and the Zoom Tool options will appear on the Option bar. Click on the + or - icons or hold down the **Alt** key to change the options from positive to negative or vice versa.*

Zooming can also be done through the **View** menu. To zoom in, go to View, Zoom In (**Ctrl++**), to zoom out go to View, Zoom Out (**Ctrl+-**), to fit an image to your screen size in one step go to View, Fit on Screen (**Ctrl+0**.)

### Correcting Mistakes - Undo, Redo

Another important feature that many programs have is Undo and Redo. If you make a mistake, a quick way to fix it is to go to the Edit menu at the top and choose the Undo option at the top of the drop down menu (Ctrl+Z). If you decide you want to Redo this step, go to the Edit menu again and choose the Redo option at the top of the menu (also Ctrl+Z). It is also possible to go to the last saved version of your document by choosing File, Revert. Or, you can access the History palette.

### History Palette

The History palette is an extremely powerful function in Photoshop®. If you do not see this palette (or window) while you are using your program, go to the Window menu and select History. (This option will go from unchecked to checked in the menu when it is activated.)

When you make a mistake and want to go back several steps, look at the History palette to see up to 20 of the most recent, previous steps. Each step, listed in the order that it was performed, corresponds with the state of the document when that step was applied. Click on one of the previous steps shown in the History palette to revert to the state that your document was in when that step was performed. If you don't want to remain at that earlier state that your document was in, you can click on a later step as long as you haven't started working on the document again. Beginning to work on the image at an earlier step in the History palette deletes all the subsequent History steps and begins recording document history again from the newly selected step.

**Important -** The History palette steps are not automatically saved when you close a file. They are available only while the file is still open.

*History Palette*

*This example of a History palette is showing the last six steps that were performed on an open file.*

**Elements**® ~ This window is called "Undo History" in Elements®, and may be accessed under the Window menu in the top Menu bar.

## Layers Palette

Layers are an essential feature of Photoshop® that allow one to keep the elements of a composition separate so they can be changed and moved independently of each other. We will use layers often in the exercises, but for now, a brief overview is called for. It is important to always be aware of layers and which layer is activated when working in Photoshop®.

When an unaltered photo is first opened in Photoshop® it only has one layer, by default. This layer is always labeled as "Background" in the Layers palette and is referred to as the Background layer.

*Background layer in Layers palette*

The little padlock icon on this layer indicates it is locked and some changes cannot be performed on it at this point. You can unlock this layer by double clicking on it in the Layers palette. A preferable option (that takes more computer memory) is to duplicate the layer and work only on a copy of the layer. This is ideal for preserving an original copy of your photo in case you ever need to go back to it. We will explain more about how to do this later.

Whenever you want to work on a specific layer, you must first always make sure that the correct layer is activated on the Layers palette. Otherwise, nothing may happen, or you might alter a layer that you did not intend to alter. If this happens, use Undo or the History palette to correct the mistake. To activate a layer, click on it in the Layers palette. The active layer is always dark blue.

Besides duplicating layers, you can make new layers in the Layers palette. There is also a place to change the opacity of a layer. There are many other features of the Layers palette but these are the ones you will use first and most often.

**Optional:  Try the examples below to understand how layers work. We will explore part of the beginning and end of a later exercise.**

**Example 1** – Duplicate a Layer

**1. From the Menu bar at the top of your screen in Photoshop®, click on File, Open.**
**2. Navigate to the <u>Photo-Imaging Pics</u> folder that you copied to your computer.**

This is the folder we will be working from in all of the exercises.

**3. Select <u>Boy-Girl-01.tif</u> and press Open.**

<u>Boy-Girl-01.tif</u>

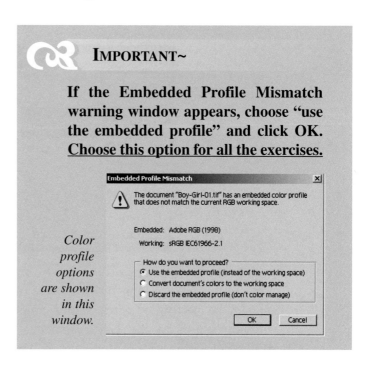

IMPORTANT~

**If the Embedded Profile Mismatch warning window appears, choose "use the embedded profile" and click OK. <u>Choose this option for all the exercises.</u>**

*Color profile options are shown in this window.*

**4. Find the Layers palette. If it is not open, go to Window on the top Menu, then choose Layers from the drop-down Menu.**
**5. On the Layers palette, click on the Background layer, hold down the mouse and drag the layer to the New Layer Icon at the bottom of the palette. Release the mouse button. A new copy of the layer will appear above the Background layer in the Layers palette.**

*Drag Layer to the New Layer Icon to copy the layer.*

*A duplicate layer is created.*

**6. Click on the New Layer Icon at the bottom of the Layers palette.**

A new empty layer will be created above the last one that is selected (shown in blue). The gray checkerboard background thumbnail in the layer thumbnail image indicates that it is empty or transparent.

*Click on the new layer icon to make a new blank layer called Layer 1 (shown above). The image of the Boy and Girl will look the same.*

**7. Click on the Move Tool in the Toolbox.**

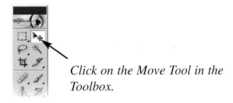

*Click on the Move Tool in the Toolbox.*

**8. Click on the layer in the layer palette labeled "Background copy" to activate it. It will turn blue on the Layers palette.**

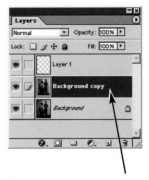

*First, activate the layer you want to work on.*

**9. Click on the photo, hold down the mouse, and drag down and to the right using the Move Tool you selected. Keep dragging the Background copy layer until you can see some of the image from the layer underneath.**

*"Background" layer*

*"Background copy" layer*
*(this layer is above the*
*"Background" layer)*

Boy-Girl-01.tif

You can see that you have moved the new "Background copy" layer with the Move Tool. The original "Background" layer now partly shows from underneath the new duplicate layer. Note that the thumbnail image on the Background layer shows the change that took place on the layer after the image on that layer was moved.

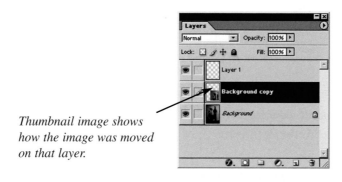

*Thumbnail image shows*
*how the image was moved*
*on that layer.*

**10. File, close. Do not save.**

**Elements®** ~ The Layers palette in Elements® displays the Layer Style icons at the top of the Layers palette, rather than the bottom, as shown in the Photoshop® palette.

## Example 2 – View a File Containing Layers

**1. Open <u>French House Sky Done.psd</u> from the Next Step Images folder on your CD, Disc Two. (This is a Next Step Image that we will be viewing.)**

**2. Find the Layers palette.**

<u>French House Sky Done.psd</u>

*Layers palette for*
<u>French House Sky Done.psd</u>

**3. Click on the eye next to the layer labeled Shadow Layer so that it disappears. Now click on the eye next to the layer named House Layer.**

*Click on the eye icon next to the Shadow layer and House layer to turn off their visibility.*

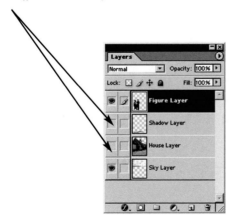

<u>French House Sky Done.psd</u>

The shadow layer under the figures and the House layer are no longer visible in the document because their visibility has been turned off in the Layers palette. More of the sky can now be seen because it is no longer partially blocked by the House on the layer above it. The bottom sky layer on the Layers palette is also the bottom layer in the document. A layer can be moved to another place in the layer order by clicking on it on the Layers palette, holding the mouse button down, and dragging it to another spot on the Layers palette.

**IMPORTANT~**

**In the following exercises, numbered items in bolder type are commands to be performed on your computer. These commands (except Color Match) may be used with all versions of Photoshop® from Version 6.0 through Photoshop® CS®. The commands are all executed through the main Menu at the top, and its drop-down menus. Where appropriate, shortcut keys are noted, which you may begin using when you become comfortable with the tools they represent.**

## Exercise #1 - Straighten a Crooked or Out-of-Square Photo
### *Trim, Skew, Selection, Polygonal Lasso*

Photographing one's artwork can be a painful process without proper lighting, light meters, slide film, angle calculations, etc., etc., etc. While most successful fine artists eventually succumb to the necessity of learning to be a more professional photographer, many painters simply do not have the equipment to take excellent, squared-up photographs of their artwork.

As long as galleries or art competitions will accept digital images in place of traditional slides, you can use Photoshop® to overcome many of the problems photographing flat artwork has presented in the past. If you are an artist who deals with art under glass, you have an especially difficult time of getting your work photographed with a professional look.

With one simple function from Photoshop®, SKEW, you can create beautiful portfolio photos of your work without expensive cameras or removing the art from under the glass.

Reflectivity off the surface of glass, or highly varnished oil painting surfaces has long been a problem for photographing paintings. Now you can photograph them from an angle to reduce the glare, and later square them up in Photoshop®.

See the typical amateur photo next, taken with a digital camera.

## 1. Open <u>Crooked Photo.tif</u>.

If I were using a photo such as this in my portfolio, I would want to remove the frame and simply show the painting. You could use the same method to include the frame, if it were important to the final image, such as showing a potential client the type of frame you would put on a painting, however, you would have to know the exact dimensions of the *outside* of the frame to square up the photograph with accurate proportions.

This portrait was painted on an 18x24 canvas, which will be an important measurement to know.

## 2. Be sure the foreground/background is set to the default setting of Black/White in the Toolbox. (See example under Step 4).
## 3. Click on the Lasso Tool in the Toolbox and hold down the mouse button until all three Lasso choices become available. Select the Polygonal Lasso Tool.

*Click and hold on the Lasso Tool until the additional lasso tool choices appear. Select the Polygonal Lasso Tool.*

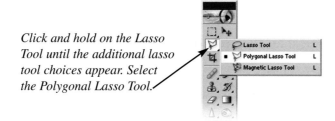

**4. Enter "0" in the Feather value box in the Options bar.**

To use the Polygonal Lasso Tool, click once on the upper left corner of the portrait, second click on the upper right corner (creating a straight line between the two points), third on the lower right corner, fourth on the lower left corner. If you click in the wrong place during this process, press Backspace, and the last point will be undone.

Finally, hover your cursor over the upper left corner where you started. Look for the small circle beside the Polygonal Lasso Tool cursor. This indicates that you can click here to close the selection. Click here now. The active selection will appear. DON'T click again! or you will start an additional selection.

*Feather value is zero*

*Polygonal Lasso Tool Selected*

*Click here to set Foreground/ Background to default Black/White*

*Just the painting is selected using the Polygonal Lasso Tool, enclosed by the "crawling line."*

You have just created a "selection" in Photoshop®. The portion of the image enclosed by the crawling line is now the only active portion of the image, and any action taken at this point will affect only the selection. This concept is at the heart of Photoshop®'s image manipulation capabilities. Being able to change some parts of an image while others remain unchanged is often entirely made possible by the "selection" function. There are countless ways to make a selection, using various tools and we will discover many of them throughout this tutorial.

**5. From the top Menu bar, press Select, Inverse.**

This will change the selected area to everything <u>outside</u> the painting image. Notice that there is now <u>another</u> crawling line around the <u>outside</u> of the entire image, as well as the original crawling line around the painted image. Since we want to <u>keep</u> the portion of this photo that represents the painting, we change the "selection" to encompass all the area <u>around</u> the painting. This is the purpose of the "inverse" command. In complex images, it is sometimes difficult to tell which portion of the image is included in the selection, so it is important to keep track of the inverse command.

**6. Press Delete to remove area around the painting.**

*The selection of the painting has been inverted to select everything but the painting. (Ctrl+Shift+I)*

*The selected area around the painting was deleted.*

**7. Press Ctrl-D to deselect the selection, or go to the top Menu bar, press Select, Deselect.**

To new Photoshop® users, forgetting to <u>deselect</u> the selection (indicated by the disappearance of the crawling line) can cause grave errors. If the program appears to "lock up" and become unresponsive to simple commands, it is probably due to your making an accidental selection that is too small for the crawling line to be visible. The program is actually responding; its actions are being performed on selections that are too small to see. So, be vigilant in keeping track of selections.

**8. On the top Menu bar, press Image, Trim to open the Trim screen. Check <u>ON</u>:**

<table>
<tr><td>**Based On:**</td><td>**Top Left Pixel Color;**</td></tr>
<tr><td>**Trim Away:**</td><td>**Top,**</td></tr>
<tr><td></td><td>**Bottom,**</td></tr>
<tr><td></td><td>**Left,**</td></tr>
<tr><td></td><td>**Right.**</td></tr>
</table>

*Select Trim Options.*

**9. Press OK.**

*Image after Trim*

This will remove all the excess background and keep the image of the painting inside a perfect rectangle. The next thing to do is straighten up the painting to fit inside the rectangle so that no white is left showing.

**(If you are skipping ahead, this step may be accessed from the file called <u>Crooked Photo-Trimmed.tif</u> in the Next Step Images folder on your CD, Disc Two.)**

10. **From Menu bar, press Select, All (Ctrl+A). We are going to edit the entire image as a selection inside a crawling line.**

11. **Click on the Maximize icon in the upper right corner of the image to enlarge it to fill the screen. (Press on it again when you want to return the image to its original view).**

*Click on the Maximize Icon, the middle icon.*

12. **Edit, Transform, Skew. Hold mouse button down and drag the upper left handle to the left until the painting aligns with the edge of the box then release mouse button. Click, hold down, and drag the right handle up until the top of the painting aligns with the box, and then drag the lower right handle down until the box is filled with the image.**

*Drag this corner upwards.*

*This corner was dragged to the left.*

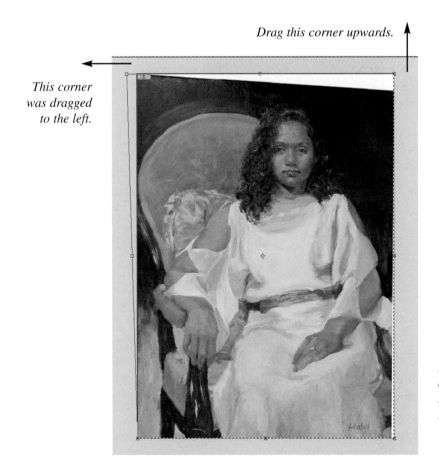

*Painting during Transform. Drag corners out to eliminate white.*

**13. Press the Enter key to accept the changes you've made.**

*Press Enter when finished with
the Transform function handles.*

**14. To be sure that nothing is still selected, go to Select, Deselect (Ctrl+D).**

*Painting after Skew*

*While the resulting photo may
look right to you, it isn't yet in
the proportion of the original
painting. Remember that the
painting was on an 18x24 canvas.
A further step is required to
assure proportional accuracy.*

**15. Select Image, Image Size from the top Menu bar and the screen below will appear.**

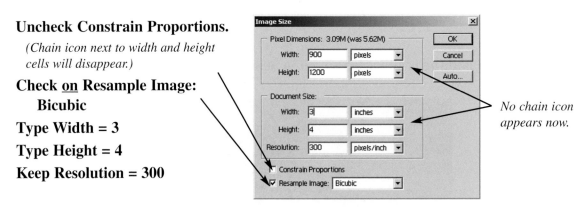

*Image Size Options. The width and height indicated above
are not in the proportions we need. An 18x24 canvas is
represented by a simple ratio of 3x4 or 6x8.*

**16. To change the figures in this screen, start at the bottom:**

**Uncheck Constrain Proportions.**
*(Chain icon next to width and height
cells will disappear.)*

**Check <u>on</u> Resample Image:
    Bicubic**

**Type Width = 3**

**Type Height = 4**

**Keep Resolution = 300**

*No chain icon
appears now.*

*Image Size Options*

**17. Press OK.**

This action will slightly widen the image compared to its length, which is now exactly the proportion of the painting. For other common canvas sizes and their respective ratios, see page 96.

*Painting after Skew*                    *Painting after Resize*

## 18. File, Close. Do not save.

**Elements**® ~ The Trim function does not exist in Elements®. Your alternative method to squaring up the photo is to complete Steps 1-7, and skip Steps 8-13. Instead, enable the Grid function (located under View on top Menu bar), and pull the handles on the image up, down, right, left until the image squares up. Then use the Rectangular Marquee Tool to select only the image of the painting. Press Image, Crop, to arrive at Step 14 in the exercise. Complete the exercise as instructed from Step 14 onward.

*( This page left intentionally blank. )*

# *E*xercise #2 - **Photographing Paintings for Publication** - *Actions Palette*

If you are photographing your work-in-progress for publication in magazine articles or art instruction books, the exercise you have just learned may make the Photoshop® program worth the price you've paid for it. Knowing you can straighten your photos after the fact can make the process of documenting your work a painless procedure. Usually, taking photos is an interruption to the painting process, and the easier you make it for yourself, the more likely you are to capture material that could be worthy of publishing in art magazines or books.

It is a fact that some artists receive more publicity in art magazines simply because they have had the foresight to photograph their work in progress, and in doing so, have become known as reliable resources for material when the magazines have a quick spot to fill in their featured articles.

While hand-held cameras can give you great results, each photo will have to be individually cropped and skewed because you'll probably never be able to photograph each frame exactly the same. The extra time it takes to resize each photo could be your undoing.

A better procedure is to set up the camera in a fixed position to include the entire image of the painting, select the highest resolution possible, and shoot each frame exactly the same. The high resolution will allow you to choose some shots later for closeup details without losing clarity of detail. If you shoot your initial photos at too low resolution, this kind of enlargement later is not feasible.

Position the camera/tripod slightly to the side of your painting position in front of the easel so you are not constantly backing into it, if you stand to paint. If seated, position the camera within arm's reach to take photos frequently during the progress of the painting. For this setup, a cable shutter release is necessary. Clicking manually can move the camera enough to prevent you from being able to use this powerful, automated tool in Photoshop®.

You needn't worry about the fact that the edges of the painting will be out of square, because you know you can straighten them later.

Once you have the photos collected for your painting in progress, you can record all the actions you perform on the first photo and apply them in a single click of the mouse to each of the succeeding photos, with very little effort. This function is performed in the Actions palette.

The Actions palette can automate any series of identical changes that you want to apply to more than one photo, not just the changes you will learn in this exercise.

**1. Open <u>Storytime-1.tif</u>, <u>Storytime-2.tif</u>, <u>Storytime-3.tif</u>, and <u>Storytime-4.tif</u>.**

These are photos I shot during the process of painting. With the camera in a fixed position, every shot was identical in size and angle. Every photo needs to be cropped and skewed exactly the same. Photoshop® provided a way to capture a set of commands and repeat them as a single command with the Actions palette.

<u>Storytime-1.tif</u>          <u>Storytime-2.tif</u>

<u>Storytime-3.tif</u>          <u>Storytime-4.tif</u>

**2. Click on <u>Storytime-1.tif</u>.**

**3. On the top Menu bar, select Windows, Actions (Alt+F9) to display the Actions screen.**

**4. Use the slider to scroll to the bottom of the list (if you have a list) on your Actions palette.**

**5. Click on the folder icon at the bottom of the Actions palette.**

*Click on the folder icon to create a new action set.*

*Enter "Storytime Actions" in the new window.*

*Actions palette*

**6. Enter "Storytime Actions" in the window that appears for the name of the new set.**
**7. Keep the set called Storytime Actions activated in blue. If it is not activated, click on it.**

We will now create an action to be stored within this set.

**8. Click on the "New Action" icon at the bottom of the screen (or click on the triangle to the right of the Action tab, and select "New Action").**

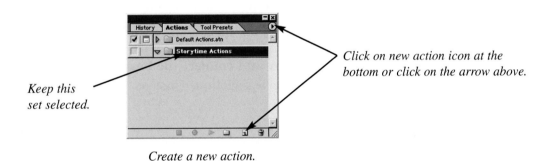

*Keep this set selected.*

*Click on new action icon at the bottom or click on the arrow above.*

*Create a new action.*

### 9. The New Action screen will appear. Type:

**Name = Storytime Resize**
**Set = Storytime Actions**
**Function Key = None**
**Color = None**

*Press Record.*

*New Action Window*

### 10. Press Record.

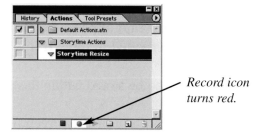

*Record icon turns red.*

*Actions palette recording*

The round button at the bottom of the Actions palette will turn red to indicate that it is now "recording" every action you make until you hit the Stop button, later.

### 11. Select Polygonal Lasso from the Toolbox and connect the four corners of the painting with straight lines to enclose a selection, (just as you did in the previous exercise #1).

If you click in the wrong place, press the Backspace key. This will undo your last click with the Polygonal Lasso Tool and will take you back to the last point that was clicked on.

**12. On top Menu bar, press Select, Inverse (Ctrl+Shift+I).**

*Selection is around the painting.*

*Selection has been inverted.*
*(Ctrl+Shift+I)*

**13. Press the Delete key.**

**14. Press Select from the top Menu bar, Deselect (Ctrl+D) to release selection.**

**15. Press Image, Trim (your settings should be the same as in the previous exercise; if not, enter the settings for Trim from Exercise #1).**

**16. Press OK.**

**17. Click on the Maximize icon in the upper right corner of the image to enlarge it to fill the screen. (Press on it again when you want to return the image to its original view).**

*Click on the Maximize Icon,*
*the middle icon.*

**18. Press Select, All (Ctrl+A).**

19. **Press Edit, Transform, Skew, and drag corners to fill the rectangle with the image of the painting.**
20. **Press the Enter key to accept the changes.**
21. **If anything is still selected, press Ctrl+D to deselect.**
22. **Press the dark gray square on the lower left of the Actions palette to stop the recording.**

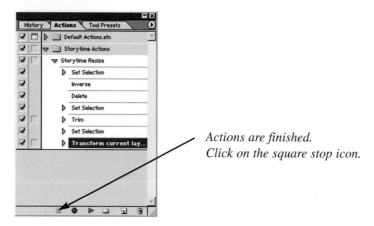

*Actions are finished.*
*Click on the square stop icon.*

You have now created an Action that can be repeated with a single click of the mouse.

23. **To be able to see the other images, click on the Minimize icon in the upper right corner of Storytime-1.tif. Minimize Storytime 4 and 3 until you have finished working with Storytime-2.tif.**

The Minimize button will make the window reduce to its title bar and it will relocate to the bottom left of your screen. The file will remain open but the image will be hidden. To return to full size, just click on the left-most icon again.

*Click on the Minimize Icon,*
*the left icon at the top of the window.*

*Storytime-1.tif window becomes minimized into*
*a bar in the lower left of the screen.*

*Click here to return image to view on screen.*

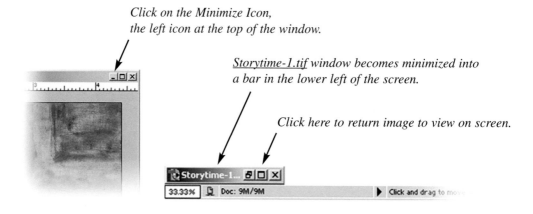

**24. Click on <u>Storytime-2.tif</u> to activate it.**

**25. Click on "Storytime Resize" on the Actions palette to activate this action.**

If you can't see it on the Actions palette, scroll up the palette using the slider on the right.

**26. Press the "Play Selection" button at the bottom of the Actions palette to start the series of automatic commands.**

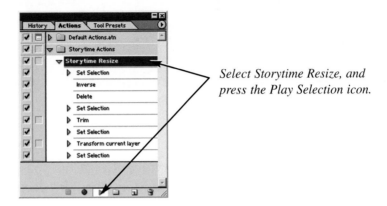

*Select Storytime Resize, and press the Play Selection icon.*

This is the button on the bottom of the Actions palette with the right arrow on it. To determine what a button does on the Action palette or the Toolbox, hover the mouse over the icon and a label will appear.

*Storytime-2.tif*  *Storytime-2.tif after Storytime Resize action*

The actions you recorded under "Storytime Resize" as you performed them on Storytime-1.tif are now applied to the Storytime-2.tif document that you are currently working in.

**27. Repeat the Storytime Resize action on Storytime-3.tif and Storytime-4.tif for more practice using actions.**
**28. File, Close, for all four files. Don't Save.**

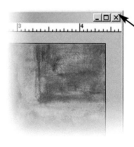

*Click on the Close icon, (the "X") on each window.*

**Elements**® ~ This function does not exist in Elements® - available only in Photoshop®.

# $\mathscr{E}$xercise #3 - **Perspective Correction** - *Skew, Guides, Rulers*

The camera has been around for almost 200 years, and photographs are so ubiquitous that we rarely question them for accuracy. We are blind to their distortions, having come to believe a photograph rather than our own eyes. This blind reliance on photographs causes grief for many painters who choose not to work from life. As soon as one learns to draw from the live model, still life setup, or outdoor setting, the inaccuracies of photography become blatant.

Most photographs of buildings are taken with a wide-angle lens, which immediately distorts the linear perspective of said buildings. The lens that gives accurate perspective is a 50mm lens with no zoom capacity. But, if you look through the viewfinder at the 50mm lens setting (on your wide-angle lens), you will see that it shows only a small portion of a wall on a building close to you. You immediately want to expand the amount of information seen in the viewfinder—and that's when you introduce distortion. Distortion of vertical walls can be corrected easily using the Skew Tool in Photoshop®. It is useful for the artist to understand what kinds of distortions occur in photographs so that they can be corrected in a convincing way.

If you have not yet learned to draw from life, then you must accept the assertion that there are perspective distortions by cameras, and be wary of the pitfalls that photographs offer.

If your camera can zoom, your photos are doomed!

There is scarcely a consumer camera on the market that does not have a zoom/wide angle feature. If you can zoom in for a closer look, then your camera has it. This is the kiss of death for accurate perspective!

As soon as you zoom out to get a wider view of a scene, you have changed the visual perspective in all the buildings in the scene. An example of this distortion can be seen by comparing a photograph of a church (Fig. 1) to a sketch of the church (Fig. 2) hand-drawn, on-site without the aid of photography.

Notice that the buildings in the photograph seem to be leaning backward, almost about to topple over. This is because I had my wide angle lens pulled out to its extreme. Even the shorter buildings seem to be falling back. Comparing the sketch-from-life to the photograph, you can see that the buildings were quite well-grounded, and not about to topple over. There *was* a slight tilt to the tower, but not as severe as seen in the photo.

*Fig. 1*

*Fig. 2*

This is the extreme that you will find in photographs, and something you must avoid introducing into your paintings. To correct a photographic distortion such as that seen in Fig. 1, you have to know at least one rule about drawing buildings. **Truly vertical surfaces must be parallel with the sides of the rectangle they are in** (canvas or photograph). If they are not, then the perspective is distorted, and you must correct it.

Less obvious, yet equally wrong, is the distortion in the perspective of the horizontal lines (edges of roofs, separations between floors of tower). Unfortunately, the only remedy for this is the ability to draw in perspective learned by on-location sketching. The angles of the horizontal roof line in the sketch are noticeably flatter than those in the photo. So, a rule of thumb would be to reduce the angles of horizontal lines to a flatter representation. This requires a judgement call by the artist and there is no rule that will automatically solve this problem — except experience in the field — and lots of sketching buildings from life.

## 1. Open <u>Todi.tif</u>.

The photograph selected for this exercise was taken in the medieval city of Todi, Italy, where the buildings have stood for hundreds of years. It was shot during an on-location workshop, with my first digital camera. For the first time, I was able to prove to my students, on the spot, that cameras distort perspective.

*Todi.tif*

In this alleyway, you can see that the farthest wall through the archway is fairly perpendicular (parallel to the edges of the photo). As you move backward, closer to where the photographer is standing, the building walls appear to lean further inward.

You might be fooled into thinking that because these buildings are so old, they actually do lean in. But they do NOT. As a lesson to the participants there in Todi, we compared the angle of the walls to a plumb line (a weighted string hung from the fingers), and all the walls were perfectly plumb (straight up vertical). None were leaning inward.

We all took turns standing where I took the photograph and comparing the walls measured with a plumb line to the image on my digital camera's tiny screen. The distortion was so obvious that even the most novice painter could see it. We might have been tempted to conclude later (if this photo had been taken on film), back in the studio, that the old buildings must be distorted, because we are so used to seeing those types of distortion in photos.

Strangely enough, however, when we see this type of distortion replicated in our paintings, even the *least* knowledgeable viewer knows that something isn't quite right about it. That's because we intuitively know what structures look like that are constructed with truly vertical walls. And, even if a painting is exactly like the photograph, it still seems inaccurate. What we will accept in a photograph, we won't accept in a painting.

**2. Click on Full Screen icon - upper right corner of image, top bar.**
**3. Click on the Move Tool in the Toolbox.**

*Select the Move Tool
in the Toolbox.*

This is an important and frequently used tool in the Toolbox that is needed for moving items and guides by clicking and dragging. This tool must also be selected before the right menu items will be available in the top Options bar for this exercise.

**4. From the Menu bar, click Select, All (Ctrl+A).**

*Selection becomes
active around the entire
outer edge of photo.*

**5. Edit, Transform, Skew - grab the upper left corner and drag to left until wall on left appears upright; grab upper right corner handle and drag right until wall is vertical.**

*Drag each top corner outward.*

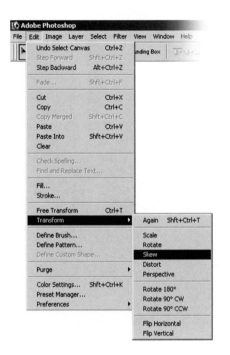

**6. Press Enter.**

You can check the vertical or horizontal alignment of things using guides in the next steps.

**7. If rulers are not already visible around your image, activate them in the Menu bar by clicking on: View, Rulers (Ctrl+R). Rulers will become visible on the side and top of the image.**

**Elements**® ~ Rulers do not exist in Elements®. Use instead the Grid function, which is activated under the View menu in the top Menu bar. Use the grid lines as your reference to pull the image into a more vertical aspect.

**8. Click on View, Show, Guides (Ctrl+;) (If there is a checkmark next to Guides, it is already activated).**

*The check mark next to Guides means that they are already turned on and available to use. (Do not select this if it is already checked or it will deactivate.)*

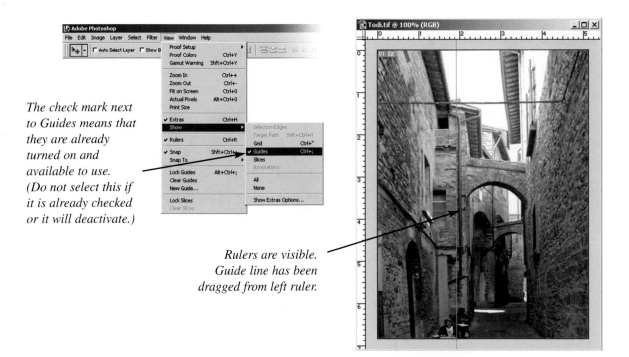

*Rulers are visible. Guide line has been dragged from left ruler.*

**9. Select the Move Tool by clicking on it in the Toolbox at left. Click inside the vertical ruler on the left side and drag the blue guide line by holding down the mouse button. A blue line "guide" will appear as soon as the mouse crosses out of the ruler into the photo. Still holding down the mouse button, drag the guide line to align with the gutter pipe and release the mouse button.**

**10. Readjust the skew of the picture again if necessary using Edit, Transform, Skew.**

**11. With the Move Tool still selected, click on the guide and drag it back to the ruler to remove it.**

**12. If the guide will not move, go to View, Lock Guides. This should unlock the guide so that you can now move it.**

**13. File, Close. Don't save (or save under a new name).**

The resulting image is more nearly what was seen in real life.

# $\mathscr{E}$xercise #4 - **Straightening Lopsided Photos** - *Rotate*

Another type of perspective problem occurs when the camera is not level, as with the photograph below. Everything looks lopsided. The problem here was caused by one of the tripod's legs sitting in a hole. Unless your tripod has a leveling bubble on it, it's easy to make this mistake. You can sometimes make this mistake with hand-held shots, as well. Fortunately, with Photoshop®, it's easy to correct with the Rotate function.

**1. Open <u>Lopsided House.tif</u>.**
**2. Be sure Rulers are turned on. If not, go to View, Rulers (Ctrl-R), and click on Rulers to place a checkmark beside it.**
**3. Pull a Guide line from the left ruler into the photo and align it with the bottom of the nearest porch post.**

Lopsided House.tif

Lopsided House.tif
*Rulers and guide*

**4. From the top Menu bar, select Image, Rotate Canvas, Arbitrary.**

**5. Type Angle = 3, check °CW (degrees clockwise), Press OK.**

This is a trial and error method of straightening a lopsided photo. You must visually compare a vertical surface with the guide to tell if you have straightened it enough. You can also compare the guide to the tree on the far left to see that it is now also standing straight up.

Now, of course, you have white edges around the perimeter of the photo, but these can be cropped out by using the Rectangular Marquee Tool to select a smaller portion of the photo and discard the rest.

*Rectangular Marquee Tool*

**6. Click on the Rectangular Marquee Tool in the Toolbox, (Feather=0) and drag a selection within the photo that does not include any of the white background.**

In the Options bar above, Feather=0. Hold down the left mouse button and pull down to right until you have enclosed the portion of the photo you want to save.

Lopsided House.tif
*after rotation*

Lopsided House.tif
*with Rectangular Marquee selection*

**7. If the selection is not exactly where you want it, go to the Select menu at the top of the screen and choose Transform Selection.**

To change a selection without changing the selected area, use the options found in the Select menu. The Transform Selection feature found here will only change the selection parameters and not the image itself.

**8. Drag the handles that appear on the selection so that the selection is positioned correctly. Press Enter.**

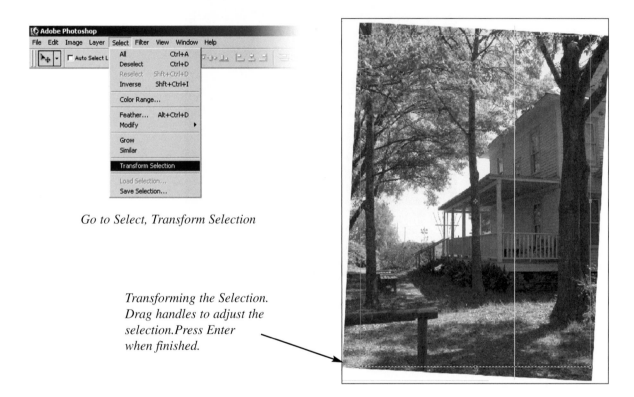

*Go to Select, Transform Selection*

*Transforming the Selection. Drag handles to adjust the selection.Press Enter when finished.*

Once you press Enter, the selection the handles will disappear and the selection will return to the active moving state that it was in.

**9. Image, Crop.**

This will automatically resize the photo to the smaller area that was selected.

**10. Select, deselect (Ctrl+D).**

**11. Click on the Move Tool and drag the guide off to the ruler on the left.**

<u>Lopsided House.tif</u>
*after Cropping*

**12. File, Close. Don't Save.**

**Elements**® ~ Perform the following instead of the Photoshop® instructions, for the steps below. Follow other steps as written.

<u>Step 2-3</u> - Enable Grid under View on top Menu bar.
<u>Step 4</u> - Select Image, Rotate Canvas, Custom.
<u>Step 5</u> - Type Angle = 3, check ºRight (degrees right), Press OK.

# $\mathscr{E}$xercise #5 - **Replace Unwanted Elements** - *Cloning*

Sometimes photographs need more than a perspective correction to make them useful. In the case of the next photo, I wanted to use it as a background for a figure painting, but the chain across the front of the picture was an element I didn't want to use. Of course, as a painter, I could just ignore it, but if I want to merge it with another photograph containing my figures, the chain and post won't make sense, so I'd really like to remove it. Also, I'd like to show it as a sunny day with a blue, cloud-filled sky, rather than the overcast day shown here. My figure subjects were photographed in bright, direct light, and I want the light to be consistent between the two photographs. So, this photo will receive several make-overs.

This image will be used in another exercise later in the program, after you have made corrections to the perspective distortions.

French House.tif

## 1. Open, French House.tif.

**2. Set Background Color as white in the Toolbox. To do this, click on the button in the Toolbox that sets the default foreground and background to be respectively black and white.**

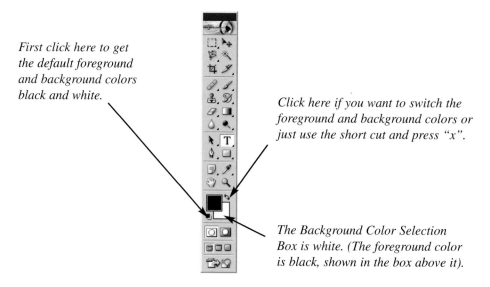

*First click here to get the default foreground and background colors black and white.*

*Click here if you want to switch the foreground and background colors or just use the short cut and press "x".*

*The Background Color Selection Box is white. (The foreground color is black, shown in the box above it).*

**3. Image, Canvas Size.**
**4. Change the number for width = 5.5 and leave the height unchanged.**
**5. Click on the correct square in the grid so that the canvas will not expand to the right. (See below)**

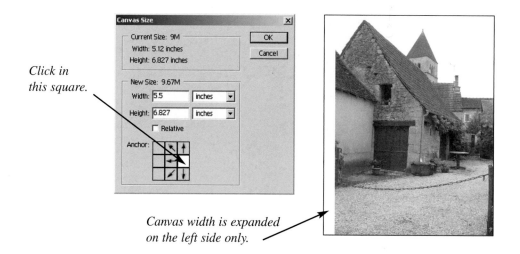

*Click in this square.*

*Canvas width is expanded on the left side only.*

This ensures that all the additional width will be added only to the left side of the image. Since we are working on the Background Layer (the default layer when opening a file) the color of the added width will be the background color. We have already set the background color to white above.

6. **Press OK.**

7. **Click on Full Screen icon.**

8. **File, Save As <u>My French House.tif</u>.**

9. **Select, All  (Ctrl+A).**

10. **Edit, Transform, Skew - Grab the upper left corner and drag to left until the corner of the gray wall on left appears upright.**

11. **Press Enter.**

12. **Select, Deselect (Ctrl+D).**

*The wall appears more upright.*

*Select Clone Stamp Tool.*

*French House after Skewing*

This is the image after skewing. It is now more upright and the lens distortion of the photo has been eliminated. We are now going to fill in the white space at the left of the building by cloning the nearby portions of the picture into it. Extra elements in the picture such as the chain will be cloned over until they are gone. First we will select the Clone Stamp Tool and choose a brush size and shape for it.

13. **Click on Clone Stamp Tool - "S."  The Clone Tool will now be indicated in the Options bar at the top of your screen.**

14. **Enter settings in the Options bar for the Clone Tool. Opacity = 100, Flow = 100, Aligned box is checked, Use All Layers box is unchecked.**

*Match the settings above for the Clone Stamp Tool.*

**15. Click on the down arrow next to "brush" on the left side of the Options bar at the top. This opens the drop down Brush Preset picker.**

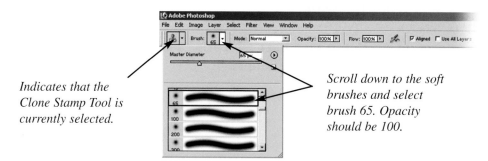

*Indicates that the Clone Stamp Tool is currently selected.*

*Scroll down to the soft brushes and select brush 65. Opacity should be 100.*

**16. Scroll down to the softer brushes and click on one labeled with a diameter of about 65 pixels. Click somewhere outside the Brush Preset picker to close it (or press the Esc key).**

You have just selected a brush size for the Clone Stamp Tool. You can change the diameter using the slider or choose a different preset brush in the Brush picker at any time while cloning in this exercise.

**17. Move the cursor over your document to see the brush size you selected. The cursor will be a circle that is the size of the brush you choose.**

After selecting the Clone Tool and its brush size, we must always designate the sample area that we want to clone from. The Clone Stamp Tool will not work until we do this. We will now designate a spot on the ground at the bottom of the picture to begin cloning from. Then we will clone the ground into the empty white area to the left. It will work best to sample near this area to get the closest matching colors and textures.

**18. Hold down the Alt key and Left-click in the stones near the bottom of the photo not too far from the white area. Then release the Alt key.**

When you hold down the Alt key, the cursor becomes a target shape. The Clone Stamp Tool has now been told to begin sampling (copying) from the area that you just clicked on with this target shape cursor. It will "remember" this spot from now on and will always clone from this same distance to the cursor until you select a different sample point using the Alt key.

*(Clone Stamp Tool is selected.)*
*Hold down the Alt key and Left-Click on the ground here to indicate that you want to clone (copy) from this area.*
*(Target shape is not actual size.)*

*French House after Skewing*

**19. Now move the cursor to the white area.**

While you are painting with the Clone Stamp Tool, the History palette remembers what is done after each release of the mouse.

**Using the Clone Stamp Tool -** Begin cloning with short slow strokes, releasing the mouse at each stroke. This way a record will automatically be created in the History palette of the stage of the image at each stroke. You can then go back to these stages in the History palette if needed.

Start out cloning in a slow motion to give the computer time to "catch up" with you before cloning more strokes. Cloning requires a lot of computer memory and may be a slow function to perform. If you go too fast, the Clone Stamp Tool may not do exactly what you are intending for it to do.

**20. Press and hold down the mouse button while moving the mouse <u>slowly</u>. You are now cloning (copying) stones into the white area from the source spot.**

*The circle indicates the brush size that is painting. The crosshairs indicate what is being copied. (not actual size)*

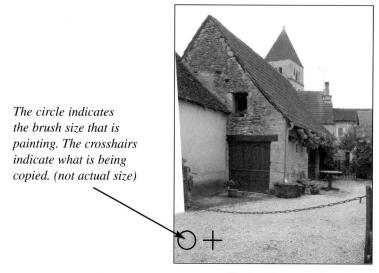

*Cloning the ground into the white area.*

While you hold down the mouse button, you can see your brush indicated as a circle and you can also see crosshairs where you are cloning (sampling) from. The crosshair area will be copied to the white area as we move the cursor over the white area. Notice that the crosshair moves in relation to where the cursor moves at every click and drag of the mouse when "Align" is checked in the top Options bar.

**21. Finish copying the ground into the white area. Clone and redesignate sample areas whenever necessary so that the texture blends into the white area in a seamless natural way.**

**22. Clone parts of the gray wall and cover the adjacent white edge on the left. Continue cloning this wall into the empty white area so that it seamlessly meets the edge of the picture.**

**23. Finish cloning the roof above the gray wall into the empty white area. All the white area should be cloned over.**

**24. Clone portions of the ground to remove the chain and the post from the image.**

*Before Skewing and Cloning*          *After Skewing and Cloning*

**(This completed image may be accessed from the file called <u>My French House.tif</u> in the Next Step Images folder on your CD, Disc Two, for use in later exercises if you were unsuccessful in your first attempts at skewing and cloning.)**

**25. File, Save (Ctrl+S).**
**26. File, Close.**

**Elements®** ~ Perform the following instead of the Photoshop® instructions, for the step below. Follow other steps as written.

<u>Step 3</u> - Image, Resize, Canvas Size.

*( This page left intentionally blank. )*

# *E*xercise #6 - **Revealing Detail in Dark Photos** - *Levels*

If you can take only one exposure of a photo, it should be underexposed to show the detail in the light areas. That is because we can reveal the detail in the deep shadows through the use of the Levels feature in Photoshop®.

The photograph seen below left was exposed to capture all the details in the light values of the white blouse. As a result, her face, which is in shadow, can hardly be seen at all. But all is not lost. You can recapture the lost detail with the Levels feature. The Levels feature controls the value relationships in the photograph by making light areas darker, or dark areas lighter.

Becky in Sun.tif
*Before Levels*

Becky in Sun.tif
*After Levels*

**1. Open, <u>Becky in Sun.tif</u>.**

**2. Image, Adjustments, Levels (Ctrl+L) - Levels screen will pop up. Check the Preview box. Channel = RGB. Grab gray input slider at center of large box and move right and left to see changes in image.**

The middle Input slider changes the brightness and darkness of the middle range of tones without affecting the highlights and shadows as much.

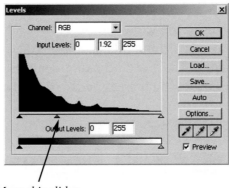

*Move this slider.*

**3. Cancel - return image to original state.**

Keep image open for next exercise.

**Elements®** ~ Perform the following instead of the Photoshop® instructions, for the step below. Follow other steps as written.

Step 2 - Enhance, Adjust Lighting, Levels.
Elements® has a quite advanced feature that automates this function better than Photoshop®. Under the Enhance menu, you can select Auto Smart Fix, or Adjust Smart Fix - for more customized control of value [levels] shifts.

# *E*xercise #7 - **Revealing Detail in Dark Photos** - *Variations*

The Variations option is a powerful feature of Photoshop® that allows you to change many variables simultaneously: value range, color cast, and color saturation. In this exercise, we will achieve the same result as we did in the last exercise—by a different method.

**1. Image, Adjustments, Variations - a large screen will appear that offers many choices.**

*Click on
Original first.*

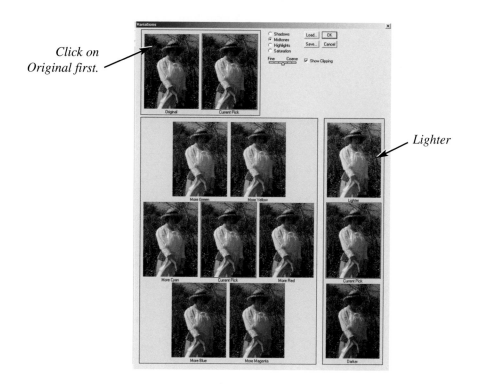

*Lighter*

**2. Left-Click on "Original" photo at top left.**

A default feature of the Photoshop® program is to apply, automatically, the color correction used the last time the Variations function was used. Always perform this action <u>first</u> unless you want to repeat a previous effect on the current photo.

**3. Click on Midtones - to change the value of colors between the lightest and darkest ones.**
**4. Click on the image "Lighter" to see the same change you created using Levels in the previous exercise.**
**5. Notice that the "Current Pick" shows the comparison between the current adjustment and the original image. If you don't like the change, click on the "Original" to revert back.**

**6. Click on any image in the group of seven on the left side of the window to see how the color is adjusted in the Current Pick.**

**7. To create smaller changes in color or value, move the slider toward "Fine."**

**8. Press Cancel to abort.**

**9. File, Close.**

**Elements**® ~ Perform the following instead of the Photoshop® instructions, for the steps below. Follow other steps as written.

<u>Step 1</u> - Enhance, Adjust Color, Color Variations.
<u>Step 2</u> - Left-click on "Before"....same settings as Photoshop®.

# $\mathscr{E}$xercise #8 - Simplifying Planes for Painting Portraits, Still Life, & Landscape - *Posterize, Grayscale, Desaturate, Tiling*

### Part A – Simplifying Facial Planes for Painting Portraits - Posterize in Grayscale

This is the single most important tool that computer-imaging programs offer to the portrait painter. Artists are taught to see the form of the head in simple planes of color and value. To the novice, this is very difficult.

One of the first things students of portrait painting are taught to see is the separation between light and shadow on the face. While this may seem to be a simple concept, it is often very illusive, especially in varying lighting situations. Because the human eye is so responsive to changes in light, a painter can completely misread an area in shadow if they stare at it continuously. A dark area can be perceived as much lighter than it really is, if peered at too long.

This is why art instructors constantly remind students to take a "quick look" or a glance at the subject, rather than prolonged staring. The quick look gives a much better representation of accurate value because the eye doesn't have time to respond by opening up and seeing too much in the shadow areas.

To further encourage students to "see in the right way", teachers implore students to constantly squint at the model rather than looking at her with eyes wide open. This suppresses the eyes' natural response of opening up and seeing more. What painters really must learn to see are the essential, simple value patterns on the face.

Until photo-imaging programs were available, painters had to rely totally on their own eyes to fathom these shapes. Photoshop® now makes it possible to see what all the painting instructors have forever been trying to get painters to observe from life.

The first and most important value distribution to see is light and shadow, <u>without</u> all its subtle variations.

## Step 1 - Posterize Three Levels

Girl-Inside.tif

**1. File, Open Girl-Inside.tif.**
**2, Image, Mode, Grayscale, Discard Color Information? = OK.**

This converts the image from color to shades of gray.

**Camera Tip -** To see the benefits of this exercise most easily, choose a photo that has only one strong light source.

**3. Save As <u>Girl-Inside-Grayscale.tif</u> and KEEP OPEN for next step.**

<u>Girl-Inside-Grayscale.tif</u>

 *Tip~*

**Using Levels** - In Photoshop®, the term "Levels" relates to the term "values" in painting, especially when using the Posterize function. When applied to a photograph, the program analyzes the distribution of values and assigns the infinite variations of shades of gray into the number of levels (values) you wish to see. Photoshop® automatically assigns the darkest values to black, and the lightest values to white, even if they are not totally black or white.

**4. Image, Adjustments, Posterize. Set Levels =3, Click Preview box on; Press OK.**

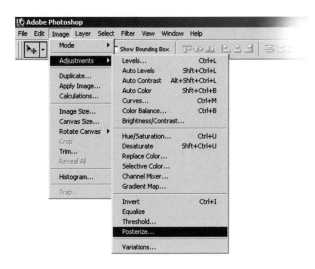

Sometimes, depending on the model's clothing, you may be able to set the Levels = 2 to achieve this separation between light and shadow on the face. As you can see in this photo, the white lace on her dress was lighter than anything on her face. If we had chosen Levels = 2, we would not have achieved an accurate value pattern. (Try it, and you'll see what happens.)

Although we see the pinpoints of highlights on her nose and forehead, the most important pattern is the separation between light and shadow on her face. The image below would be most useful for the initial lay-in of paint to establish the dark value shape on the face. You would not use black, of course, for the shadow pattern, but you could use a single color of paint, such as Raw Umber, to capture the heart-shaped pattern on her face, as well as the shape of her eye sockets, nose and lips. This is the first (and most important) step to getting a likeness.

Girl-Inside-3 Levels.tif

**5. Save As <u>Girl-Inside-3 Levels.tif</u>.**
**6. File, Close.**

**Elements**® ~ Perform the following instead of the Photoshop® instructions, for the step below. Follow other steps as written.

<u>Step 2</u> - Filter, Adjustments, Posterize....same settings as Photoshop®.

## Step 2 - Posterize Six Levels

What usually confuse painters are the variations within these two planes (light and shadow). In the light, you should keep your values limited to only three: highlight, light and halftone. Those pesky halftones (areas in light, just before turning into shadow) are the ones that usually sink a painting, because we invariably interpret them too dark. The shadow planes should be limited to two values, dark and reflected light, both of which are <u>always</u> <u>darker</u> than <u>any</u> of the values found in the light plane. To observe this more complex value distribution, do the following:

**1. File, Open <u>Girl-Inside-Grayscale.tif</u>. (This file was created earlier in this exercise).**
**2. Image Adjustments, Posterize - Levels = 6, Click Preview box on; Press OK.**

*Before Posterize*

*After Posterize to 6 levels. The face has three levels of light values and two levels of dark values.*

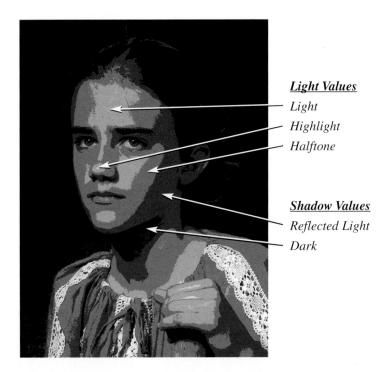

*Light Values*
*Light*
*Highlight*
*Halftone*

*Shadow Values*
*Reflected Light*
*Dark*

The 6-level posterized image now gives us useful information, as painters. We can clearly identify the lightest areas of flesh and see that they are divided into three distinct values. The highlight value (seen as a dot on the tip of the nose), the light value (cheek, chin, and forehead), and the most puzzling of all, the halftones.

The shadow planes contain two basic values: the darkest (seen on the neck under the chin, eyebrow and eyelashes) and the reflected light area (right side of face, eye sockets and ear). Nowhere in the reflected light area can you see any value as light as those values on the front, heart-shaped area in light. As long as you remember to keep these areas separate (by value), you will be able to paint a convincing head with a good likeness.

*Tip ~*

**Posterization with Six Levels -** This is really the most valuable tool for portrait painters, as it eliminates the confusion that color interjects into the perception of value by the artist.

**3. Save As <u>Girl-Inside-6 Levels Gray.tif</u>**
**4. File, Close**

**Squinting** - Just as these exercises help painters to get a simplified view of their subject there is also an older, more traditional method to do this. Painters often squint their eyes while looking at their subject in order to identify the most important values and shapes. This technique does not eliminate the element of color but it is the original method for this essential part of the painting process. A view of an image without the distracting details gives the painter the big picture of what has to be done. Details can be added later and are more for the final stages, if they are to be included at all.

*View before squinting.*
*More detail is visible.*

*View while squinting.*
*The main value areas are*
*more obvious.*

**Elements**® ~ Perform the following instead of the Photoshop® instructions, for the step below. Follow other steps as written.

<u>Step 2</u> - Filter, Adjustments, Posterize....same settings as Photoshop®.

## Part B – Simplifying Planes for Painting the Still Life - Posterize, Desaturation

These tools are as useful and effective for the Still Life painter as for the portrait painter. One mistake still life painters often make is losing sight of the big value relationships in their setups. The most powerful paintings are those which keep the big values simple. In the setup below, we see large areas of light (the white cloth and white ceramic bowl), middle (yellow pitcher and brass bowl), and dark (paisley cloth and cherries).

Using the Posterize function to see where each object fits into the value composition is a very useful reminder to the painter to keep the values close within a given range. The most helpful reference is not the color posterization; instead, the desaturated posterization is more valuable.

Why? Because we frequently view color as having a value different than it really is. Compare the color and grayscale posterized images to see that there are really far fewer value differences than there are color differences.

This exercise can help you, as a painter, to begin to see that color has the power to suggest a value change where there really is none. And this is a powerful tool the painter can use to expand the limited number of values one can make with mere pigment. Paint can never replicate the values seen in nature because it simply doesn't have the value range within it. To expand that range, we have to make use of the visual magic that color gives us to suggest a change in value when we can't actually make a value change.

**1. Open <u>Still Life Setup.tif</u>.**

**2. Image, Adjustments, Posterize, Levels = 4, press OK.**
**3. File, Save As <u>Still Life Setup-Posterize.tif</u>.**
**4. Image, Adjustments, Desaturate.**
**5. File, Save As <u>Still Life Setup-Posterize Desaturate.tif</u>.**
**6. Open <u>Still Life Setup-Posterize. tif</u>.**

> **(If you are skipping ahead you can open <u>Still Life Setup-Posterize Desaturate.tif</u> and <u>Still Life Setup-Posterize.tif</u> from the Next Step Images folder on your CD, Disc Two.)**

**7. Window, Documents, Tile (This is in version 7. If you have version CS you can go to Window, Arrange, Tile instead).**

This will fit the two images on your screen automatically so that they can be easily compared.

**8. If the images need to be reduced in viewing size, click on the Zoom Tool in the Toolbox and select the negative magnifying glass icon in the Options bar. Click in the picture to zoom out and repeat as needed.**

Compare the posterized version with the grayscale version and see that there are fewer real value changes than color changes. It is most evident on the yellow pitcher where the two colors on the light side are the same value, but the change in saturation and temperature of the yellow appears to be a value change when it is not. The same thing happens in the shadow area of the pitcher. The two colors on the shadow side are not different values, just different hues and temperatures.

*Still Life Posterized to 4 Levels*          *Posterized version after Desaturation*

Viewing the composition in its desaturated form approximates what you would see if you squint down very hard to see the setup in real life.

**9. Close both files. (In version CS you can go to File, Close All).**

**Using Photos to Work from Life** - The hardest thing for the painter to do is simplify. Until now, the squint has been the only way for one to accomplish this. And, it is still the easiest and quickest method to see what is in front of you with the live model. This book should never be construed as pushing you to work from photos rather than from life; indeed, quite the contrary. You can use photos to remind you what to look for in life.

If you are fortunate enough to have a teacher constantly at hand, and attend workshops on a monthly basis, then you probably don't need this advice. But, if you are a painter who is able to attend a workshop only once a year, or less, and have no reliable teacher to give you good direction or instruction, then you can become your own teacher with the assistance of Photoshop®.

To stay on track with your still life paintings (painted from the live setup), take photos at the beginning of your painting session. Go ahead and begin your drawing and initial lay-in of color and work until you normally take a break. Then, and only then, take your photo of the setup to Photoshop® and perform the actions suggested in this exercise. Compare the desaturated (grayscale) image of your posterized setup to your actual painting, and see if you have accurately identified the value relationships when working from life.

Becoming your own best critic is essential to recognizing and being able to correct mistakes in value relationships for the realist painter. To create the illusion of three-dimensional form on a flat surface, you must understand and express accurate value relationships. To make a pleasing three-dimensional composition with visual power, you must be able to relate the big values in the setup to each other realistically.

But what if you still can't tell if value is your problem? It's simple. Take a photo of your painting and desaturate it. Then compare the grayscale photo of your painting to the grayscale photo of the setup. The differences should be strikingly obvious, and you will know immediately where you need to focus your corrections.

**Elements®** ~ Perform the following instead of the Photoshop® instructions, for the steps below. Follow other steps as written.

Step 2 - Filter, Adjustments, Posterize....same settings as Photoshop®.
Step 4 - Enhance, Adjust Color, Remove Color.
Step 7 - Window, Images, Tile.

## Part C – Simplifying Planes for Painting the Landscape - Posterize, Desaturate

As in the previous step of this exercise, I encourage you to use photographs as a corroborative assistant to your sketches from life, rather than a substitute. Photographs can never give the emotional sense of a place that a sketch or drawing from life can give. Used during the painting process, or after the fact, photos can enlighten and suggest where problems might exist that you didn't see any other way.

The most important aspects of the landscape to capture are the relative value relationships between the largest masses in the painting. Excluding man-made elements, the natural world has a specific value order that humans intuitively understand, whether or not they are artists. Any viewer can look at a landscape painting and tell if it does not follow this natural order. They may not be able to describe how it differs, but they definitely know when it is not obeyed. From thus comes the oft-repeated comment, "I don't know what's wrong; I just know it isn't right."

*Tip ~*

**Natural Values in the Landscape** - The value patterns of the landscape are determined by nature and her atmospheric conditions, and you cannot escape this truth. Basically, there are four values in a landscape (excluding snow, sand, and water). They are:

1. Lightest value is the sky (giver of light)
2. Light value is ground (flat, horizontal plane—greatest light receiver)
3. Middle value is mountain/hill plane (presents oblique plane to the light—receives less light)
4. Darkest value is tree plane (the vertical, or upright, plane—receives least amount of light)

Defy these values, and your work will look amateurish. For an in-depth study and discussion of why these relationships exist, refer to John F. Carlson's book, *Guide to Landscape Painting*, which has been the bible for modern landscape painters for over 60 years.

Sand, snow and water present exceptions to the above value relationships in predictable ways, so learning the exceptions to the Big Four above is as essential as learning the Big Four. Describing how each is an exception is out of the purview of this book, but I encourage you to study these natural relationships as a pre-requisite to landscape painting.

**1. Open <u>Landscape.tif</u>.**

This landscape has the four big planes mentioned above: Sky, Ground, Hills, Trees. To see if they conform to the Big Four value masses, we'll follow the process of the preceding examples in the portrait and still life.

**2. Image, Adjustments, Posterize, Levels = 4, Press OK.**
**3. File, Save As <u>Landscape Posterize.tif</u>.**
**4. Image, Adjustments, Desaturate.**
**5. Save As <u>Landscape Desaturate.tif</u>.**
**6. Open <u>Landscape Posterize.tif</u>.**

**(If you are skipping ahead you can open <u>Landscape Desaturate.tif</u> and <u>Landscape-Posterize.tif</u> from the Next Step Images folder on your CD, Disc Two.)**

**7. Window, Documents, Tile (or in version CS, Window, Arrange, Tile).**

*Landscape.tif posterized to 4 levels*
(<u>Landscape Posterize.tif</u>)

*Landscape Posterize.tif after desaturation*
(<u>Landscape Desaturate.tif</u>)

8. **If the images need to be reduced in viewing size, click on the Zoom Tool and select the negative magnifying glass icon. Click in the picture to zoom out and repeat if needed.**

In looking at the color posterized version of this photo, you might be tempted to conclude that the sky is darker than the distant field. This is a perfect example of how we misread value when we are presented with differences in temperature of colors. The warm earth of the field looks lighter to us than the cool blue of the sky.

Compare the true value of the sky and distant field in the desaturated version of the photo. Clearly the sky is lighter now. Still not convinced? Try this exercise to prove that the sky is lighter than the distant ground.

9. **Activate the Eyedropper Tool on the Toolbox. Click in the sky portion of the photo and note the color and value indicated in the foreground box on the Toolbox.**

*Select the Eyedropper Tool from the Toolbox. Click on the sky part of the landscape and then the ground part of the landscape to sample and compare their values.*

*sky value*

*ground value*

Landscape Desaturate.tif

*The sampled value appears here in the foreground color box.*

Every plane in the landscape has variations of value within it. In this photograph, the grayscale image of the sky and distant mountains read as single values, respectively. The tree and ground planes, however, each have more than one value within them.

There are some values in the ground plane that are as dark as the trees, but overall, if the ground values could be expressed as a single value, it is clear that value would be lighter than the trees. Also, there are some highlight values in the near foreground that read lighter than the sky value, but they are not so light as to make the entire ground plane read as light as the sky. In fact, if you look closely, you will see that both the extreme dark and light values in the ground plane are found in the near foreground, not in the distant ground plane (where we sampled with the eyedropper for comparison with the sky). That distant plane is more nearly the single average value of the ground than either the dark or lightest values in the foreground.

There are values in the tree plane that are close to those in the distant mountains. But, if you sample them with your eyedropper and compare them with the mountain value, you'll find that the tree values are darker than the mountains.

By now, you will be thinking of all kinds of exceptions to the relationships presented above. And, there are millions of them. Just remember—there will always be exceptions to the rule, and never a contradiction of the rule. I have found that if a student continually seeks to contradict this natural relationship (or rule), rather than embracing it, they frequently fail to grasp the natural order in the world and are unable to represent it on canvas, in paint. Search for all the ways your composition can demonstrate this pattern, and your paintings will be more powerful for it.

**10. Close both files.**

**Elements® ~** Perform the following instead of the Photoshop® instructions, for the steps below. Follow other steps as written.

Step 2 - Filter, Adjustments, Posterize....same settings as Photoshop®.
Step 4 - Enhance, Adjust Color, Remove Color.
Step 7 - Window, Images, Tile.

# $\mathcal{E}$xercise #9 - Simplifying Facial Planes for Painting
### *Posterize in Color*

In the beginning, five values may be all that are necessary to get an accurate, three-dimensional likeness and drawing of a subject. When beginning to paint, however, the color temperature in a given light or shadow plane is very important to capture. The results of posterizing reveal that there are <u>more</u> <u>temperature</u> <u>changes</u> <u>than</u> <u>value</u> <u>changes</u> within a given plane. As in the grayscale exercise, I have found that a Levels value set to "6" in the Posterize function will reveal the most information to paint from.

**1. File, Open <u>Girl-Inside.tif</u>.**
**2. Image Adjustments, Posterize - Levels = 6; Click Preview box on; Press OK.**
**3. Edit, Fade Posterize - change:**
> **Opacity = 50%,**
> **Mode = Normal,**
> **Preview box on, Press OK.**

*Step 1 - Open File*  *Step 2 - Posterize*  *Step 3 - Fade Posterize*

**4. File, Save As <u>Girl-Inside-FadePosterize.tif</u>.**
**5. Close file.**

The Posterize function in Photoshop® is a brutal weapon when used for color, and must be adjusted to make fleshtones appear more natural. The Posterize command averages not only value but color into discreet planes. As painters, we should not presume that the colors in Step 2 are the exact colors we should paint from, but the image at this stage is quite useful in telling us the color family and temperature we should start with to mix accurate fleshtones.

80

The Fade Posterize function (at 50% value) actually provides a 50/50 mix between Step 1 and Step 2, so the colors seen in the individual planes are more closely related to actual paint colors we could mix to paint this face.

In the Step 3 photo (on preceding page), one very important piece of information Photoshop® gives us is the temperature of the light source illuminating the subject. The largest, lightest planes on this face display a cool temperature relative to the hot colors seen on the cheek, nose and outer forehead. Capturing this temperature shift will make your painted portraits quite life-like. The reason the temperature is cool in this photo is that the model was lit with a 5000K light, quite a bit cooler than a standard household bulb.

**Painting Theory vs. Computer Analysis -** You might wonder why you should even consider the grayscale posterized image from this exercise when beginning to paint, because the color image offers so much more information. Actually, the color version sometimes has too much information, if you are not vigilant in identifying whether a certain value plane is in light or in shadow. That's when you need the grayscale image to use for comparison.

The darker halftone that joins the lighted plane of the face to the shadow plane is the most misunderstood value on the face. It is often (incorrectly) treated as part of the shadow plane because it appears to be so different from the redder cheek area. When you compare these two areas on the grayscale image, however, it is plain to see that the two are essentially the same value, and the perceived difference is really a temperature shift, rather than a value shift.

If you must make a mistake in the value of the halftones, always paint them lighter than you think they are, never darker, because the halftones are part of the lighted side of the face, not the shadow. Likewise, always paint the reflected light on the shadow side darker than you think it is, not lighter. Misreading these value differences is usually the cause of failed portrait paintings, and missed likenesses.

To paint more powerful portrait paintings, try to keep your values simple, and make a clear distinction between light and shadow. The colors you use to paint the fleshtones can be in any color family and not affect the likeness. The values, however, are critical to getting the likeness and creating a head that looks three-dimensional.

*Posterized Grayscale Photo*                    *Posterized Color Photo*

**Elements**® ~ Perform the following instead of the Photoshop® instructions, for the steps below. Follow other steps as written.

<u>After Step 1</u>, do the following: Right-click on "Background" layer in Layers Palette, select "Duplicate Layer" and a screen will pop up that says "Background Copy". Press OK. Background Copy layer will be highlighted in dark blue in the Layers palette.
<u>Step 2</u> - Filter, Adjustments, Posterize...same settings as Photoshop®.
<u>Step 3</u> - Click on the "Opacity" slider at top of Layers palette and slide to 50%.
This takes the place of the "Fade Posterize" function, available only in Photoshop®.

*( This page left intentionally blank. )*

# *Ɛ*xercise #10  - **Adjusting Color for Portraits** - *Color Range, Lasso*

Posterization is wonderful for delineating the separate values and colors in fleshtones, but it falls short of giving us true colors, especially for the shadow areas. All flesh is alive, and while it may be illuminated with a cool light in the shadows, the colors seen in your computer printouts are hardly the colors an artist would use. This is the point where experience in painting from the live model is absolutely necessary. We will alter the shadow colors on this face by adding red and yellow, giving the colors in shadow those of living flesh.

The photo selected for this exercise is considerably cooler in overall tone than the one for the previous exercise (where the colors for all the flesh areas seemed to be usable with no alterations). This subject seems to have purple, blue, and green tones on the shadowed area of the face, a color range that will prove difficult for the computer to interpret for use as a painting reference. Fortunately, Photoshop® provides a way to correct specific areas of color without changing other areas (which are correct).

The Color Range feature will allow us to select only those colors on the face which need to be altered (namely, the shadow planes). The eyedropper is used to select the colors in the image you want to change. You can use the eyedropper on the original photo, or on the black and white image in the Color Range screen, to choose the colors that need to be changed; but it is usually easier to sample directly from the photo.

Girl-01.tif

*Girl-01.tif after posterization*
(Girl-02.tif)

1. **File, Open <u>Girl-01.tif</u>.**
2. **Image, Adjustments, Posterize - Levels = 6, Click Preview box On; Press OK.**
3. **Edit, Fade Posterize - change:**
   > **Opacity = 50%,**
   > **Mode = Normal,**
   > **Preview Box = On.**

4. **File, Save as <u>Girl-02.tif</u>.**

> The painter will immediately see that the simple planes identified on this photo by the Posterize function are those shapes that will be used in the first steps of paint application on the face. But the colors would not be attractive, as they are unnaturally cool in the shadows.

5. **Select, Color Range - Select: Sampled Colors, Fuzziness = 25.**

> The number you type in, or choose using the slider for Fuzziness, determines how many colors will be selected that are close to the color you pick with the eyedropper. Larger numbers include more colors, smaller numbers include fewer colors.

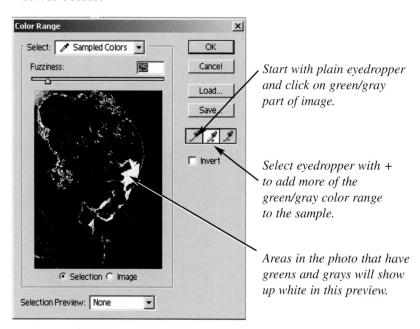

*Start with plain eyedropper and click on green/gray part of image.*

*Select eyedropper with + to add more of the green/gray color range to the sample.*

*Areas in the photo that have greens and grays will show up white in this preview.*

6. **Choose the plain eyedropper. Click on a portion of the flesh in the actual photo that appears green or gray. You may have to move this screen if it pops up and covers the image.**

> The areas you select in the photo will show as white on the Color Range preview screen.

**7. Select the eyedropper in the center with the (+) under it to add colors to your selection. Click on other green or gray colors in the actual photo.**

All the green or gray colors should now be indicated in white on the preview screen.

**8. Press OK.**

A crawling line will outline the selected colors on the original image that are indicated in white on the preview screen. Only those colors contained inside the crawling line will be affected by future color changes.

We only want certain skin tones to be selected but some of the hair and clothing may become selected with the crawling line because those areas contain some of the same colors found in the fleshtones. We do not want to adjust the colors in any of the hair or clothing so we must remove these areas from the selection using the Lasso Tool.

The Lasso Tool can be used to select an area by dragging a circle around it. A crawling line results. It can also be used to remove part of a current selection or add to a current selection.

**9. Select the Lasso Tool in the Toolbox by clicking on it or by pressing "L" to select it.**

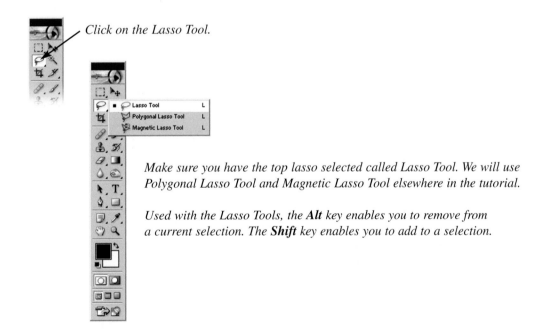

*Click on the Lasso Tool.*

*Make sure you have the top lasso selected called Lasso Tool. We will use Polygonal Lasso Tool and Magnetic Lasso Tool elsewhere in the tutorial.*

*Used with the Lasso Tools, the **Alt** key enables you to remove from a current selection. The **Shift** key enables you to add to a selection.*

10. **Hold down the Alt key. This will add a negative sign next to your cursor which means that you will be subtracting from the current selection.**

11. **While holding the Alt key, drag a circle around an area in the hair or clothing that you wish to eliminate from the selection. Eliminate any area from the selection that is not part of the skintones to be adjusted.**

    (To drag a circle you must hold down the left mouse key. Make sure that you complete the circle.)

12. **Continue drawing circles around areas you want to eliminate while holding down the Alt key.**

    If you don't hold down the Alt key, the selection will be lost and a new one will begin. Use Undo to get your original selection back if you need to. To use Undo, go to the top menu and choose Edit, Undo (Ctrl+Z). If the mouse was clicked more than once since the mistake, the History palette can still be used to get back a lost selection.

13. **Select, Modify, Smooth - Sample Radius=4, Press OK.**

    This makes the selection line less jagged and includes pixels next to the selected area by expanding 4 pixels outward.

14. **Image, Adjustments, Variations - Click on Original, Midtones, slide the Fine Course slider into the middle (if it isn't already), More Red, OK.**

    This is where the color correction to the fleshtones actually takes place.

15. **Select, Deselect (Ctrl+D).**
16. **File, Save As <u>Girl-03.tif</u>.**
17. **File, Close.**

---

**Elements**® ~ Perform the following instead of the Photoshop® instructions, for the steps below. Follow other steps as written.

<u>After Step 1</u>, do the following: Right-click on "Background" layer in Layers Palette, select "Duplicate Layer" and a screen will pop up that says "Background Copy". Press OK. Background Copy layer will be highlighted in dark blue in the Layers palette.
<u>Step 2</u> - Filter, Adjustments, Posterize...same settings as Photoshop®.
<u>Step 3</u> - Click on the "Opacity" slider at top of Layers palette and slide to 50%.
There is no comparable tool in Elements® for the "Select Color Range" function in Photoshop®. Alternatively, to accomplish the same thing, do the following to replace
<u>Steps 5-12</u> - Click on Magic Wand in Toolbox. Set Tolerance = 32, Check Anti-alias ON, Check Contiguous ON in Options bar. Hold down the Shift key while clicking with the Magic Wand in the areas that have greens and grays on the posterized face.
<u>Step 14</u> - Enhance, Adjust Color, Color Variations.......same settings as Photoshop®.

*Before*
Girl-01.tif

*After Posterization*
Girl-02.tif

*After Fade Posterize,*
*& Color Adjustment*
*of green/gray appearing*
*flesh areas (Girl-03.tif)*

*( This page left intentionally blank. )*

# Exercise #11 - Seeing Color in Shades of Gray
*Desaturate, Adjustment Layer*

You have seen the benefit of looking at your photograph in grayscale, and that the Mode change is a quick, one-step method of converting color to shades of gray, but it requires you to save your image as a different file in order to preserve your original color image.

Another way to view your photograph, as either color or grayscale, is to use the Desaturate feature on an Adjustment Layer in the original color photo file. This is a non-destructive method of achieving virtually the same thing, while keeping both color and grayscale images within the same file. As you accumulate more and more images, you will find that keeping all the variations of a single project image together is a filing chore. Saving your file in layers eliminates the possible separation of all the variations.

An adjustment layer is a useful tool because it does not cause a loss of data in the original image. Its effects can be turned on or off at will, without changing the file. In this exercise, we will see that we can view (or print) the image in either color or grayscale by one click of the mouse, within the same image file.

**1. Open <u>Girl-01.tif.</u>**
**2. Window, Layers - "F7" to activate Layers palette (if it isn't already visible).**

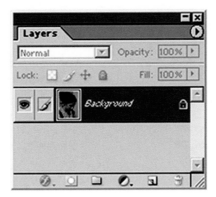

### 3. Layer, New Adjustment Layer, Hue/Saturation.

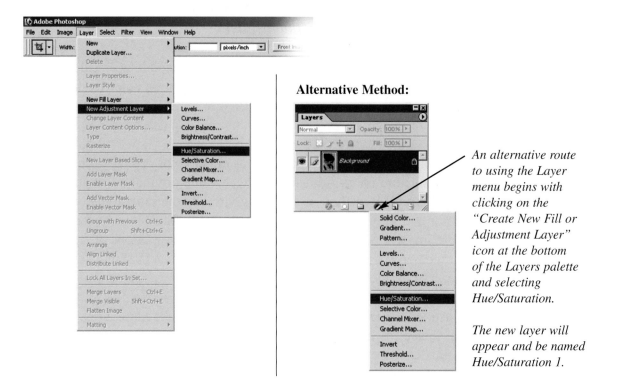

**Alternative Method:**

*An alternative route to using the Layer menu begins with clicking on the "Create New Fill or Adjustment Layer" icon at the bottom of the Layers palette and selecting Hue/Saturation.*

*The new layer will appear and be named Hue/Saturation 1.*

A screen will appear with the Name = Hue/Saturation 1. Press OK. A new layer will appear in the Layers palette with this name and the Hue/Saturation screen will appear.

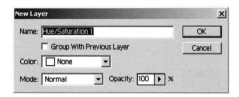

*New Layer Window, Press OK (Skip this step if you used the alternative method above).*

*New adjustment layer is created in the Layers palette.*

**4. Drag the slider under Saturation all the way to the left. Press OK.**

The color will be removed from the image.

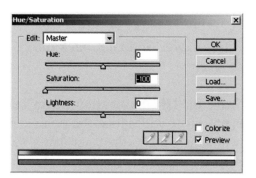

*Hue/Saturation Window*

<u>Girl-01.tif</u> *after desaturation*

**5. Click on the eye icon next to the Hue/Saturation 1 Layer to turn it off.**

See that the image returns to color. To print both color and grayscale images from this file, simply turn the eye icon on or off, depending on which you wish to print.

*Layers Palette*
*Click on eye icon next to the*
*adjustment layer to turn it off.*

<u>Girl-01.tif</u>
*Adjustment layer is turned off.*
*Image returns to color.*

You may use an adjustment layer to posterize an image as well. In previous exercises, we posterized each image and saved them to new separate files. This time, we will create a posterizing adjustment layer, that can be turned on and off (just like the desaturating adjustment layer) so additional files will not have to be created. The new posterizing adjustment layer will now allow us to see this image in either posterized color or posterized grayscale.

**6. Click on the eye next to the Hue/Saturation Layer to turn it back on.**
The image is black and white again.

**7. Select the Background layer again or leave the Hue/Saturation Layer selected.**
Either way, the next adjustment layer will adjust the color of the background layer. The adjustment layer will appear above the layer that is selected and affect the first layer beneath it that has an image (the background layer in this case). If there were other layers beneath the adjustment layer, they would all be affected, so you need to be aware of this effect in your own future work on photographs.

**8. Layer, New Adjustment Layer, Posterize.**
A new Posterize window will open with Name - Posterize = 1. Press OK.
The Posterize Levels window will open, asking for the number of levels (values) you want to view.

**Number of Levels to Use** - The useful number of levels chosen for any image depends on the specific image. While 6 levels is generally a good number to choose, 5 or 7 levels might be more informative. The way to determine exactly how many levels will reveal the most information for any photo is to first view it as a 3-level image. This will reduce the image to only light and shadow, with perhaps a smattering of white highlights elsewhere in the photo. When posterizing faces, if there are any values in the photo lighter than the face, those areas will appear as white, and the lighted area of the face will appear as middle value, while the shadows will appear black.

The simplest shapes of the light/shadow pattern on the face are the ones you are looking for at this stage. Next, you should try entering in the Levels box, numbers 5, 6, and 7. Whichever of these gives you the closest light/dark pattern to the Value 3 distribution is the one you would choose.

**9. First, enter Levels = 3 (without pressing OK) and observe the light/dark pattern on the image. Then backspace and enter the number 6 and view the difference. Backspace again and enter the number 7.**

The three different images should look like these. Which of the latter two look more like the Levels = 3 image?

Girl-01.tif
*Posterization Levels = 3*

Girl-01.tif
*Posterization Levels = 6*

Girl-01.tif
*Posterization Levels = 7*

Remember, the most important information you need is which colors/values fall into the light portion of the face, and which fall into the shadow portion.

**10. After entering Levels = 7, press OK to accept this value.**

**11. Click on the eye icon next to the Hue/Saturation 1 layer to turn it off, and you can see the posterized version of the image in color.**

Girl-01.tif
*Posterization Levels = 7*
*Hue/Saturation layer is turned off.*

Girl-01.tif
*Posterization Levels = 7*
*Hue/Saturation Layer is turned on.*

Clicking this layer on and off will show you that there are more colors within a single value area than you think. In the dark values, the reddish color at the edge of the shadow is really the same value as the gray-green area. In color, the gray-green area looks darker, but that is only the effect of temperature on our perception of value. If you ever wanted proof that temperature affects how we perceive color, this will illustrate it.

**(If you are skipping ahead, this step may be accessed from the file called <u>Girl-01 AdjustmentLayers.tif</u> in the Next Step Images folder on your CD, Disc Two.)**

**Basic Color Theory for Painters -** Warm colors are perceived as being lighter in value than they really are. Cool colors are perceived as being darker in value than they really are. Photoshop® can illustrate the <u>true</u> relative values of warm and cool colors within a value plane.

**12. Save image as a TIFF with layers using the same name <u>Girl-01.tif</u>.**

If you save this file with the .psd extension, you will have made an additional file on your hard drive. Saving the file as a TIFF with layers will prevent you from inadvertently adding more files to your system than necessary. Because you have made all the changes in adjustment layers, you can turn them off at any time and view, print, or import to another program, the original file on the background layer.

You can decide which adjustment layers you would like to have <u>ON</u> (with the eye icon activated and the layer showing) before you save and import the file to another program. If you want to use the image of the file with the Hue/Saturation layer turned on, for example, make sure that this layer is turned on and save the file as a TIFF (with or without layers). Then when you import (or insert) the image into a document page in another program such as Word, the image will appear as it was when you saved it.

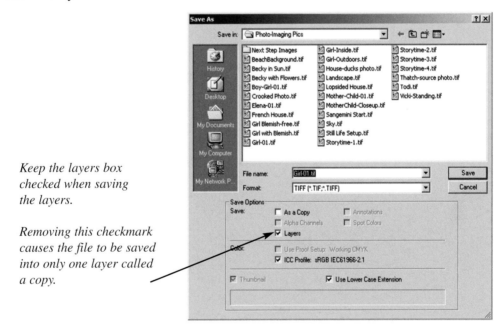

*Keep the layers box checked when saving the layers.*

*Removing this checkmark causes the file to be saved into only one layer called a copy.*

**13. File, Close.**

**Elements**® ~ Perform the steps exactly the same as in Photoshop®.

*( This page left intentionally blank. )*

# Exercise #12 - Tools for Converting Color to Gray
## *Desaturate vs. Grayscale Mode*

As a painter, I have used both tools to turn my color images into grayscale. While they may seem to do the same thing, they do not. Each averages the values differently, and they do not produce the same results. Converting a color image from RGB mode to Grayscale mode permanently deletes all color information, and must be saved as a new file to preserve the original color image. Also, posterizing a grayscale image will give you a subtly different value pattern than posterizing a color image, and then desaturating, to produce grayscale. To prove a point, this exercise will compare both functions.

You will be the ultimate decision maker on which method of converting to gray you wish to use in your work. I prefer Desaturation, but you may prefer Grayscale mode. There is no right/wrong choice in this.

**1. Open <u>Girl-03.tif</u> (from where you saved it earlier).**

(If you are skipping ahead, this step may be accessed from the file called <u>Girl-03.tif</u> in the Next Step Images folder on your CD, Disc Two.)

**2. Image, Adjustments, Desaturate.**
**3. Save As <u>Girl-04 Desaturate.tif</u>.**
**4. Open <u>Girl-03.tif</u>.**
**5. Image, Mode, Grayscale, Press OK.**

*Girl-03.tif after Desaturate*
(Girl-04 Desaturate.tif)

*Girl-03.tif after Grayscale*
(Girl-04 Grayscale.tif)

It should be obvious that the halftones are where the real difference comes into play. And, as I said previously, the halftones are where most painters will fail. Therefore, I would choose the desaturated image which makes the halftones lighter, rather than darker. In this example, the desaturate function shows the halftones lighter in relative value than the grayscale mode does. The area in question is the lower cheek, which presents a very oblique surface to the light source, yet is still considered in the light plane. In the Grayscale image, it is unclear if this area is in light or in shadow. This might seem not to make much difference to the casual observer, but to painters, the difference is great.

**6. Save As <u>Girl-04 Grayscale.tif</u>.**
**7. Close both files.**

**Elements**® ~ Perform the following instead of the Photoshop® instructions, for the step below. Follow other steps as written.

<u>Step 2</u> - Enhance, Adjust Color, Remove Color.

# ℰxercise #13 - Change Key and Color Cast - *Variations*

Often, a painter wants to paint an overall light-value-range painting (high key), or skew the color scheme to something that is entirely believable, yet painted in an unnatural color scheme. Using the Variations feature, you can accomplish both, or either, effects quickly and easily. With the previous exercise, you could paint a portrait quite faithfully by following the values and colors suggested by the computer. Try the following changes to see equally useful color schemes and key variations.

**Part A** – **Variations for Portraits**

**1. File, Open <u>Girl-03.tif</u> (again from where you saved it).**
**2. Image, Adjustments, Variations - Choose: Click on Original, Select Midtones, Slide the Fine Course slider to the middle, Lighter, Lighter.**
**3. Press OK.**

This will put the fleshtones into a higher value range, yet maintain their relative values so that you keep the likeness.

<u>Girl-03.tif</u>
*Before Lighten*

<u>Girl-03.tif</u>
*After Lighten*

**4. Image, Adjustments, Variations - Click on Original, Move the Fine/Course slider one notch towards fine. Choose: Midtones, then click on any color variation to shift the color cast.**
**5. Press OK.**

Any of the color options you choose will offer a different color cast to the image, and if you follow the suggestion of the image preview, you can create imaginative color schemes that work!

**6. File, Save As <u>Girl-05.tif</u> - only if you want to, File, Close.**

**Elements**® ~ Perform the following instead of the Photoshop® instructions, for the step below. Follow other steps as written.

Step 2 - Enhance, Adjust Color, Color Variations (Use "Before" instead of "Original").

**Part B** – Variations for Landscapes

**Example Color Schemes: Four Variations of a Photo Taken in Sangemini, Italy.**

*Original Photo*

*Yellow Added*

*Red Added*

*Blue Added*

1. **Open Sangemini Start.tif.**
2. **Try different color variations by adding yellow, red, or blue.**
3. **Save if you wish.**
4. **File, Close.**

# *E*xercise #14 - **Fitting Photo to Standard Canvas Size** - *Crop*

As with many effects, you can crop an image more than one way. The Crop Tool allows you to set the dimensions exactly as you wish the end-size of the image to be. It also allows you to move the selection box around within the image until you capture everything you want, without resorting to using the rulers at the top and left side of the screen. No rulers on your screen? They can be enabled through the View menu on the top Menu bar (Ctrl+R).

Let's crop the photo in this exercise to a standard 16x20 inch canvas size. The Crop Tool not only crops the photo; it also enlarges it simultaneously to the same (16x20) size and changes the resolution. The Crop function does it all at once without having to use several, separate tools.

The original photo has a resolution of 300ppi, but the large working copy that we are creating, which can be used to paint from, will only have to be 72ppi. It will still have enough detail to paint from at this large 16x20 size. Because we scanned it in originally at a high resolution, we are able to enlarge it greatly without losing too much image quality.

**1. File, Open, <u>Becky with Flowers.tif</u>.**

<u>Becky with Flowers.tif</u>
*(6.4w x 8.533h, 300ppi)*

<u>Becky with Flowers.tif</u>
after cropping
*(16w x 20h, 72ppi)*

**2. Select Crop Tool (C) - On the Options bar at the top of your screen, type: Width = 16 in, Height = 20 in, Resolution = 72 pixels/inch.**

The picture will be enlarged greatly, so we are lowering the resolution. Lowering the resolution to 72 ppi will prevent the file size from becoming too large to manage, which could slow down the performance of your computer.

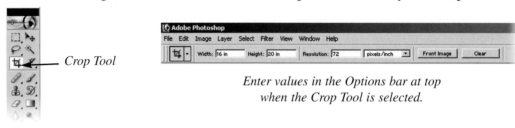

— Crop Tool

*Enter values in the Options bar at top
when the Crop Tool is selected.*

**3. Place cursor at upper right of image and drag down toward the left. <u>Any place you stop will give you the proportion of a 16x20 canvas.</u>**

When you release the mouse button, the area outside of the selected image turns dark gray. You can move the crop box by putting the mouse in the middle of the image, and while holding down the left mouse button, reposition the boundary box wherever you like. Use the arrow keys if you want to move the box only a small amount. The corner handles can be dragged to adjust the amount of the image that the crop box covers.

(If you would like to crop the photo freehand, without any proportional restraints on the crop box, delete any dimensional values indicated in the Options bar above when the Crop Tool is selected.)

**4. Press Enter to accept the change - <u>this action enlarges the print size of the file to the canvas size you have chosen.</u>**

**5. KEEP OPEN for the printing instructions in the next exercise or save as <u>BeckyFlowers-Cropped.tif.</u>**

To keep the file size small and the resolution high, use these width/height ratios (at 300 ppi) for the most common sizes of canvas:

| Common Ratios | Corresponding Canvas Sizes (common full sizes) |
|---|---|
| w=5, h=6 | 20x24, 25x30, 30x36 |
| w=4, h=5 | 8x10, 16x20, 24x30 |
| w=3, h=4 | 9x12, 18x24, 30x40, 36x48 |
| w=2, h=3 | 20x30, 24x36 |

**Elements®** ~ Perform the steps exactly the same as in Photoshop®.

# $\mathcal{E}$xercise #15 - Printing Large Photos on Small Printers
## *Guides, Rectangular Marquee*

Perhaps you are doing a larger painting and you would like a full sized printout of what you are going to paint. If your printer only prints letter or tabloid size, you still have the option of printing out parts of the photo separately and then assembling them into one big print.

Most printers print within a defined print area that does not reach the edge of the paper. In that case, it is necessary to divide up the photo into sections that are small enough to print within this area. There is usually about a quarter inch margin around the edges. Some inkjet printers leave a quarter inch margin on three sides and a half inch margin on the bottom.

Taking these things into account, the approximate print area on a letter size piece of paper is most likely going to be **8x10 (inkjet) or 8x10.5 (laser printer)**. A tabloid print area will be around **10.5x16 (inkjet) or 10.5x16.5 (laser printer)**.

### Part A – Printing a 16x20 Photo on Letter Sized Paper

We will first divide the 16x20 inch photo into four equal 8x10 inch sections using Guides.

1. **Continue with <u>BeckywithFlowers.tif</u> from the last exercise if it is already open. If it is not open, you can open the file saved from the last exercise called <u>BeckyFlowers-Cropped.tif</u>.**

   **(This step may be accessed from the file called <u>BeckyFlowers-Cropped.tif</u> in the Next Step Images folder on your CD, Disc Two.)**

2. **Ruler must be on (View, Rulers, or Ctrl+R).**
3. **Click on Move Tool.**
4. **Hold the left mouse button down inside the vertical ruler and drag out a guide line into the picture.**
5. **Continue to drag the guide across the photo and release when it reaches the 8-inch mark on the horizontal ruler at the top of the photo.**
6. **Then, hold the mouse down inside the horizontal ruler at the top and drag down another guide line until it reaches the 10-inch mark on the vertical rule at the left, release mouse button.**

*Drag Guides out from the rulers.*

*This action divides the 16x20 image into four 8x10 images that will match up perfectly when printed separately.*

Now we will select and print each of the four sections separately.

**7. Make sure Snap to Guides are on: View, Snap To, Guides (Guides will be checked if it is already on).**

This will allow you to select each section easily without having to wonder if you've captured each quadrant perfectly. It also prevents overlap of the sections in the final image when assembled into one large print. Photoshop® does not yet have an automatic tiling feature to perform this function, but this simple method allows you to easily create large prints with any type of printer.

**8. Select the Rectangular Marquee selection tool in the Toolbox and drag a rectangle over the top left quadrant created by the Guides. The selection should snap to the edges of the guides.**

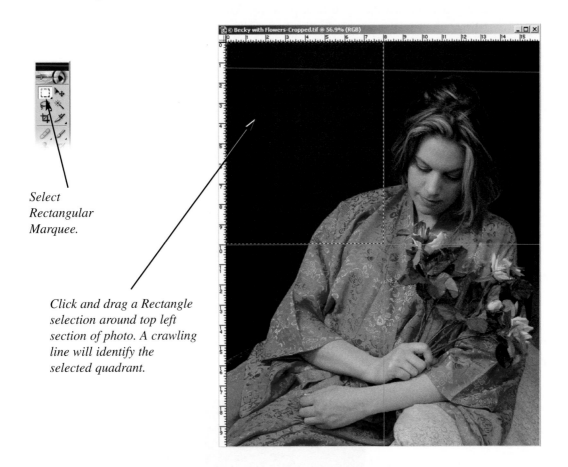

*Select Rectangular Marquee.*

*Click and drag a Rectangle selection around top left section of photo. A crawling line will identify the selected quadrant.*

Since you are making the selection while rulers are turned on, it may be easier to begin the selection from the center of the photo. Then you will avoid creating extra guides.

**9. Choose File, Print. Under Print range, "Selection" should be marked rather than "All".**

Printers vary in their print screens, so yours may look different than this one, but every printer has the option of printing All, Variable Pages, or Selection only. For tiling, always choose "Selection".

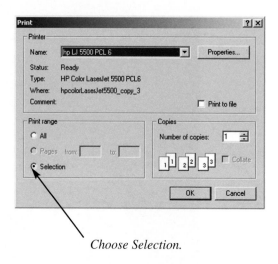

*Choose Selection.*

**10. Printer should be set to print vertically (Portrait) on Letter size paper.**
**11. Press OK.**

*Only the top left section printed.*

**12. Keep active the rectangle selection you made. With the Rectangular Marquee Tool still selected in the Toolbox, click and drag in the center of the active selection. Position the rectangular selection into a new quadrant.**

Notice that the selection "snaps" to the guides easily.

The Marquee Tool will move a selection box without moving the piece of the image that is selected. If you unintentionally use a different tool from the Toolbox something else can happen. If you had used the Move Tool from the Toolbox to move the selection, the selection <u>and</u> the portion of the image selected would have both been moved and your photo would have been rearranged. You can try this yourself with the Move Tool selected. Click and drag on the selection and see what happens. To go back to where we were, go to Edit, Undo (Ctrl+Z) or use the History palette (by clicking on an earlier stage).

 *Right!*

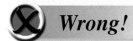 *Wrong!*

*The Rectangular Marquee Tool was used to move the Selection.*

*The Move Tool was selected in the Toolbox instead of the Rectangular Marquee Tool.*

13. **Print this section the same way as the last and continue selecting and printing the remaining two sections.**

14. **Select, Deselect (Ctrl+D)**

15. **Trim the edges off the paper and attach the four sections to make the full sized photo printout.**

16. **Now remove the vertical guide in the photo by dragging it to the vertical ruler using the Move Tool.**

17. **KEEP FILE OPEN for the next exercise.**

> If you are not going to print on 11x17 paper in the next exercise, you can close the file and don't save.

## Part B – Printing a 16x20 Photo on Tabloid Sized Paper

We will first divide the 16x20 inch photo into two equal 16x10 inch halves that will fit on 11x17 inch paper. The horizontal guide line is already in place if you did the last exercise.

*Horizontal Guide*
*for printing on 11x17 paper.*

*First print on 11x17 paper is*
*from the top half selection.*

**(If you did the last exercise, skip steps 1–6).**

**1. Open <u>BeckyFlowers-Cropped.tif</u> if it is not already open.**

(This file is available in the Next Step Images folder on your CD, Disc Two.)

**2. Ruler must be on (View, Rulers, or Ctrl+R).**

3. **Click on Move Tool.**
4. **Hold the left mouse button down inside the horizontal ruler and drag down into the picture.**

   A blue line "guide" will appear as soon as the mouse crosses out of the ruler into the photo.

5. **Continue to drag the guide down the photo and release when it reaches the 10-inch mark on the vertical ruler on the left side of the photo.**
6. **Make sure Snap to Guides are on: View, Snap To, Guides (Guides will be checked if it is already on).**
7. **Select the Rectangular Marquee Tool.**
8. **Drag a selection around the top half of the photo marked by the guideline.**
9. **Choose File, Print.**

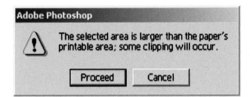

*A warning may appear to let you know that the selected paper size is too small for the selected print area. Press proceed and then adjust the selected paper size in the step below.*

10. **Under Print range, "Selection" should be indicated rather than "All".**
11. **Choose 11x17 sized paper and set printer to print horizontally (Landscape).**
12. **Press OK.**

   The selected top half of the image will print.

13. **Keep the rectangle selection you made active. With the Rectangular Marquee Tool still selected in the Toolbox, click and drag in the center of the active selection. Move the rectangular selection to the bottom half of the photo.**

   The selection "snaps" to the guides easily.

14. **Choose File, Print. Under Print range choose Selection. Printer should be set to print horizontally (Landscape).**
15. **Select, Deselect (Ctrl+D).**
16. **Remove horizontal guide by dragging it to the top with the Move Tool.**
17. **Close and don't save the file or save it under another name.**

**Elements®** ~ There is no function in Elements® that will allow the ease of printing tiled sections of a large image, as seen in Photoshop®. You may enable the grid function in Elements® to help achieve these results, but it is trial and error, at best.

*( This page left intentionally blank. )*

# ℰxercise #16 - **Removing Background**
### *Layers, Eraser, Magic Wand, Lasso, Magnetic Lasso,*
### *Polygonal Lasso, Adjustment Layer*

Rarely do you find the perfect composition in a photograph with all the elements you want. But often, you may have several different photographs that you could incorporate into one composition. The next exercise will use all the skills you have learned from previous exercises and introduce several other Photoshop® features.

The copy and paste keyboard shortcuts, (Ctrl+"C") for copy and (Ctrl+"V") for paste, are demonstrated in the following exercises. These two shortcuts are especially good to know because they are common to many computer programs and are used frequently.

## 1. File, Open Boy-Girl-01.tif.

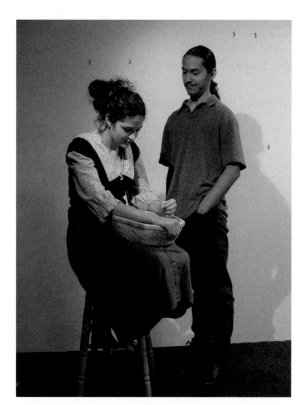

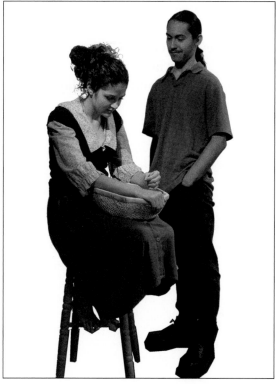

Boy-Girl-01.tif

*Background will be erased like this.*

**2. Window, Layers - "F7" to activate Layers palette (if it isn't already visible).**

We are going to make a duplicate of the original Background layer containing the photo and then work on the Background <u>copy</u> layer. A white layer will be placed under the Background copy layer so that it will show through when part of this copy layer is erased.

**3. Layer, Duplicate Layer - Give the layer a new name "Erase". (Another method to duplicate the layer is to drag the layer over the "create a new layer" icon on the layer palette. See diagram).**

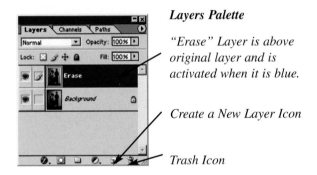

*Layers Palette*

*"Erase" Layer is above original layer and is activated when it is blue.*

*Create a New Layer Icon*

*Trash Icon*

**4. Layer, New Layer (or Click on "Create a New Layer" Icon on Layer palette to create a new layer).**
**5. Double click on name of new layer and enter name "White Background."**

**6. Click on default color button on Toolbox.**

Background will be white and foreground will be black on palette.

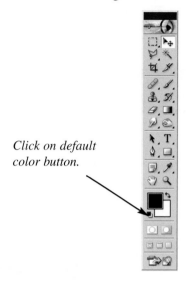

*Click on default
color button.*

**7. Edit, Fill, choose "Background Color" from drop down menu (With White Layer still in background on Layers palette). Click OK.**

Layer will become white. Ctrl + "backspace" also fills layer with background color.

**8. Grab White Layer in Layers palette and pull down under the "Erase" layer so that the white background is between the lower layer image and the upper layer image.**

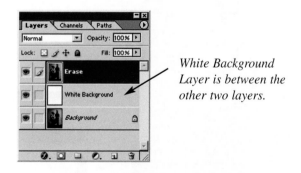

*White Background
Layer is between the
other two layers.*

**9. Click on "Erase" Layer on Layers palette to activate it.**

**10. Click on Eraser Tool - (E) - On the Toolbox at the top of the screen, change the following values: Mode=Brush, Opacity=100%, Flow=100%. Click on the brush palette that drops down from the right side of the Options bar at the top. Select "Brush Tip Shape". Change Diameter to 100 and change Hardness to about 85%. Click off brush palette to collapse it.**

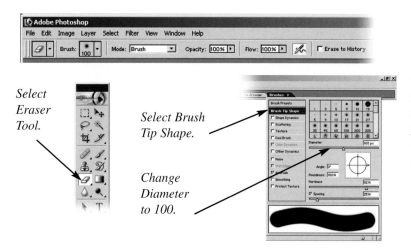

*Select Eraser Tool.*

*Select Brush Tip Shape.*

*Change Diameter to 100.*

*This drop down palette is from version 7.0 of the Adobe® Photoshop® program and varies among versions of the program.*

**11. Erase background around figures by holding down left mouse button. Get close but not touching figures. This is a gross cut. If you make an error: Edit, Undo Eraser. The Undo key command is (Ctrl+ Z).**

*Erasing with "Erase" layer selected.*

**(This step may be accessed from the file called <u>Boy-Girl Step11 Layers.psd</u> in the Next Step Images folder on your CD, Disc Two.)**

**12. Click on Zoom Tool, Select the positive magnifying glass icon on the Options bar - Click on girl's head for very closeup view.**

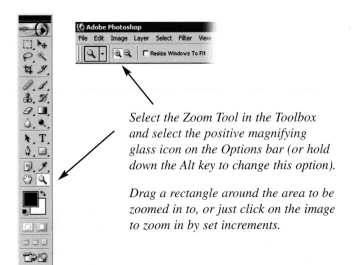

*Select the Zoom Tool in the Toolbox and select the positive magnifying glass icon on the Options bar (or hold down the Alt key to change this option).*

*Drag a rectangle around the area to be zoomed in to, or just click on the image to zoom in by set increments.*

*Closeup of Girl's Head. Use Magic Wand to delete background here.*

Another way to use the Zoom Tool (when + is selected) is to click and drag it to form a rectangle around the area that you want to zoom to. That area will become large on the screen once you release the mouse button.

To view the whole image on screen again, choose View, Fit on Screen (Ctrl+0). Fit on Screen often comes in handy.

13. **Select Magic Wand - set Tolerance = 15 and check ✓ Contiguous, ✓ Use All Layers, and ✓ Anti-aliased (these are on the bar at the top of the screen). Click on an area of background surrounding the girl's head and hair. An area will now be selected.**
14. **Hold down the Shift key to add to the selection with the next click with the magic wand. Now click on more areas of the background around the girl's head. Release the Shift key.**
15. **Hold down the Alt key to remove from the selection if needed. Click on any areas of selection that should not be there. Release the Alt key.**
16. **Press the delete key to clear what is in the selection. The white layer will show from underneath.**
17. **Select, Deselect. (Ctrl+D) Repeat above steps as necessary to eliminate gross areas.**

*Use Magic Wand to select background very close to girl's head and hair; then delete. Best for areas where the background contrasts greatly with the figures.*

*Using Magic Wand to delete the background.*

*Use Erase Tool to eliminate unwanted artifacts.*

18. **Take care not to delete some of the clothing that may be the same color as the background. You can deselect portions of clothing using the Lasso Tool and the Alt-left button function.**
19. **Click on Erase Tool, click on brush size on top bar and change to 10.**
20. **Continue to erase carefully around the outer edges of the figures. We will erase the lower center, dark areas later.**

**21. Click on the eye-icon in the Layers palette beside the White Background layer to turn the visibility off. This allows you to see down to the original background layer.**

*Eye icon turns layer on and off.*

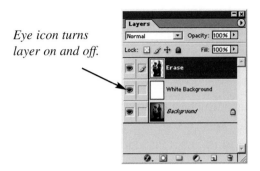

**22. Compare what is left on the layer you are working on with the Background layer. Turn the white layer visibility on and off as necessary. Check erasures to be sure you haven't erased important shapes.**

**23. If you have erased important shapes, choose Edit, Undo erase (Ctrl+Z) or use the History palette to back up several steps.**

*Background around outer edges of figures is erased.*

In this exercise using an adjustment layer, we will lighten the darkest areas around the feet so the shapes can be seen clearly while we erase the background around them.

**24. If the White layer is not visible, activate it by clicking on the eye icon next to White Background Layer in the Layers palette. The Erase layer should still be activated in blue on the Layers palette.**

We are going to continue working on the Erase layer to remove the background from the figures. We need to be able to distinguish the boy's feet from the dark floor at the bottom. Since we don't want to lighten the Erase layer permanently, we will create a temporary adjustment layer.

Later when we are finished removing the background floor from around the boy's feet on the Erase layer, we will delete the adjustment layer. The color of the Erase layer will return to its original, darker color.

**(If you are skipping ahead, this step may be accessed from the file called <u>Boy-Girl Step24 Layers.psd</u> in the Next Step Images folder on your CD, Disc Two.)**

**25. With Erase layer activated on the Layers palette, create a new adjustment layer. From the Layers palette, click on the New Adjustment Layer icon at the bottom and select Levels. (To use the Layers menu instead, go to Layers, New Adjustment Layer, Levels).**

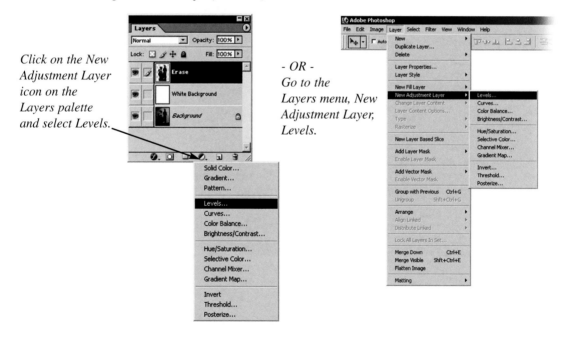

*Click on the New Adjustment Layer icon on the Layers palette and select Levels.*

*- OR -*
*Go to the Layers menu, New Adjustment Layer, Levels.*

**26. If you used the New Adjustment Layer icon on the Layers palette, skip to step 27. If you used the Layer menu, a window appeared asking for the Layer name. Press OK and the default name "Levels 1" will be given.**

*Press OK.*

**27. On the window that appears for Levels, drag the middle triangle to the left until Input Values read: 0, 2.5, 255. Press OK. This lightens the image enough to see into the dark areas around the figures.**

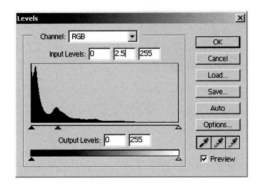

*Enter Input Values:*
*0, 2.5, 255*
*Then press OK.*

**28. The new adjustment layer called Levels 1 will be created above the Erase layer and it will also be selected on the Layers palette. Select the Erase layer again on the Layers palette by clicking on it.**

*New adjustment layer appears above the Erase Layer.*

*Select Erase layer again by clicking on it.*

*Photo now looks lightened and lower*
*shapes can be distinguished better.*

29. **You may want to preserve your work, and the layers you created, before going any farther by saving the file as a Photoshop® document (".psd") or a TIFF file (".tif") with layers.**

    If you have enough memory on your computer for larger files with layers, save as <u>Boy-Girl-02.psd</u> or <u>Boy-Girl.tif</u> but make sure to preserve the layers since we aren't finished with them yet (layers box should be checked <u>on</u> in menu while saving). One way to keep track of which files have layers and which don't is to always save layered files as a ".psd" (Adobe® Photoshop® document) and flattened files always as ".tif".

30. **Click on the Zoom Tool.**
31. **Zoom in on the area of background above the floor and the boy's feet.**
32. **Click on Magnetic Lasso.**

    The Magnetic Lasso works especially well for selecting areas in which the background contrasts greatly with the figures. We will be selecting the area of gray background near the feet of the figures with the Magnetic Lasso Tool because it contrasts greatly with the figures and floor nearby. Once the selection is finished and ready as an active crawling line, we will delete this area from the figure layer.

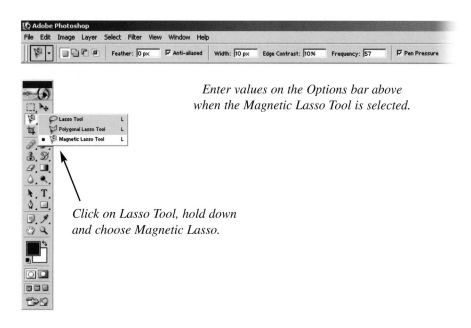

*Enter values on the Options bar above*
*when the Magnetic Lasso Tool is selected.*

*Click on Lasso Tool, hold down*
*and choose Magnetic Lasso.*

**33. Set the options in the Option bar for the Magnetic Lasso Tool. Feather = 0, check Anti-aliased, Width = 10px, Edge Contrast 10%, Frequency = 57.**

**Feathering** is set at zero because we do not need a soft edge.

**Anti-aliased** will help to keep the edges from looking rough or pixelated so that will be checked. (Pen pressure does not apply to what we are doing and can be left checked or unchecked).

**Width** specifies the distance from the pointer that an edge can be detected.

**Edge Contrast** determines the minimum amount of contrast in an edge before it will be detected. Values must be between 1% and 100%.

**Frequency** specifies the rate at which anchor points called fastening points will occur while dragging the Magnetic Lasso Tool. More will be explained later on these features.

**34. Click the Magnetic Lasso Tool somewhere on the edge of the central patch of white background near feet of the figures (see following picture).**

This will create the first fastening point. Fastening points anchor the selection border that will be created as the tool is dragged.

**35. Drag the pointer along the edge of the dark figures, stool, and floor where it meets the white background area (as in following picture).**

When using the Magnetic Lasso Tool, keep in mind that you must eventually complete a circle by returning to your starting point. The mouse button does not have to be held down.

*Magnetic Lasso Tool in use on area of high contrast.*

*Once circle is complete selection will appear. Press Delete.*

As the pointer is traced over the desired edge and the selection border appears, fastening points will appear. Fastening points will occur according to the frequency entered in the Options bar. The selection border with fastening points will continue to appear while the mouse is dragged until the first fastening point (starting point) is reached and clicked on or until the ESC key is pressed. If the border does not snap to the correct edge, click to add an additional fastening point. This is helpful when you want to make sharp turns that the automatic tool can't "see."

To remove the last fastening point and return to the previous fastening point, press the Delete key. The Delete key may be pressed repeatedly to delete each previous fastening point until they are all gone. To remove all of the selection border at once and start over, press the ESC key.

**36. Complete a circle with the selection border by returning to the starting point where the first fastening point is. Click on this point and a crawling selection line will appear.**

Once the pointer is over the starting point, a small circle will appear next to the pointer. The small circle indicates that this is the circle closure point. Click here to complete the selection and the selection will become a smooth crawling line, as seen in other types of selections.

When we are selecting a high contrast edge, we can use a higher Width and a higher Edge Contrast. This allows our tracing of the edge to be rougher yet effective. If we are tracing an image with softer edges, it is preferable to use a lower width and edge contrast. The edge must be traced more precisely in this situation.

**37. Press delete to erase the contents of the selection.**
**38. Select, deselect (Ctrl+D).**
**39. Click on the Zoom Tool and select the negative tool from the Option bar at the top.**
**40. Zoom out a little so that the entire floor is shown large on the screen (Ctrl + "-").**

*Erase areas of low contrast manually with Eraser Tool (or use the Polygonal Lasso Tool in the Toolbox).*

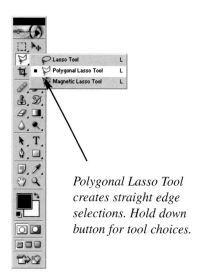

*Polygonal Lasso Tool creates straight edge selections. Hold down button for tool choices.*

**41. Select Polygonal Lasso Tool - Do this by clicking on the Lasso Tool and holding the mouse button down until the extra fly-out menu appears. Choose the second lasso labeled Polygonal Lasso.**
**42. Click around stool legs with straight lines to define the area containing the rug (to be deleted).**

**43. Complete a "circle" with the Polygonal Lasso Tool selection by going back to the starting point.**

When the pointer is over the starting point, a small circle will appear next to it indicating that this is the circle closure point.

**44. Click on the starting point. A crawling line will appear.**
**45. Delete.**
**46. Select, Deselect (Ctrl+D).**
**47. Make "Background" layer invisible by clicking on the eye next to it. We will preserve this original layer in case you want to go back to it later.**
**48. Double click on the name "Erase" on the Erase layer in the Layers palette and enter the new name "Figure Layer."**

(If you are skipping ahead, this step may be accessed from the file called Boy-Girl-02-Light.psd in the Next Step Images folder on your CD, Disc Two.)

Now that we have finished removing the background from the Figure Layer (which was the Erase layer) we would like it to return it to its original level of darkness. We will now delete the adjustment layer above the Figure Layer.

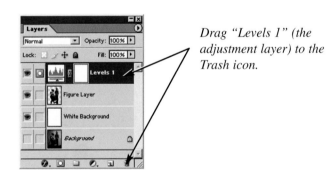

*Drag "Levels 1" (the adjustment layer) to the Trash icon.*

*Dark floor is erased.*

**49. On the Layers palette, click on the Levels 1 layer, which is the adjustment layer, and drag it to the Trash icon. (Or select Levels 1 on the Layers palette, then Layer menu, Delete, Layer). The Figure Layer looks darker again because the adjustment layer is no longer affecting its appearance. The Figure Layer has retained its original value range.**

*Adjustment layer is gone.*

*The original color and values on the Figure Layer are visible.*

**50. In the Layers palette, turn off the visibility of the White Background Layer by clicking on the eye icon next to it. The checkered squares show that the background is transparent.**

*Only the "Figure Layer" is visible.*

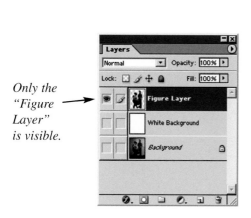

*Layers palette.*

*Final Image of Boy-Girl
Only the Figure Layer is visible.*

51. Optional - You may delete the White Background layer. Click on the White Background
    layer and drag to trash. Deleting unnecessary layers reduces the file size.
52. Save as <u>Boy-Girl-02.psd</u>. DO NOT CLOSE. Keep this file open for the next exercise.

(If you are skipping ahead, this step may be accessed from the file called <u>Boy-Girl-02.psd</u> in the Next Step Images folder on your CD, Disc Two.)

**Elements**® ~ Perform the steps exactly the same as in Photoshop®.

# &#x2130;xercise #17 - **Merging Two Photographs** - *Move, Transform*

Now that you've learned how to use many of the basic tools in Photoshop®, let's put some of the images together to make an entirely new image.

**1. File, Open <u>My French House.tif</u>.**

Both images below (<u>My French House.tif</u> and <u>Boy-Girl-02.psd</u>) should be open on screen.

**(This version of the French house may also be accessed from the file called <u>My French House.tif</u> in the Next Step Images folder on your CD, Disc Two, along with <u>Boy-Girl-02.psd</u>.)**

**2. Click on <u>Boy-Girl-02.psd</u>.**
**3. Make sure "Figure Layer" is activated.**
**4. Select Move Tool on the top of the Toolbox.**

*Move Tool*

**5. Click and drag "Figure Layer" of <u>Boy-Girl-02.psd</u> into the French House document window that is open. The figures will automatically appear on a new layer named Figure Layer in the French House document when the mouse button is released.**

Another method is to use Copy and Paste. You can copy the picture and then paste it elsewhere. To do this, go to the <u>Boy-Girl-02.psd</u> document with the Figure Layer active, Select, All (Ctrl+A) then Edit, Copy (Ctrl+C). Then click on the <u>My French House.tif</u> document and Edit, Paste (Ctrl+V). The figures will show up on a new layer called Layer 1. Double click on the name Layer 1 in the Layers palette and rename to "Figure Layer."

**6. Save as <u>My French House.psd</u> (or <u>My French House.tif</u>) and KEEP OPEN.**

**7. Close the file called <u>Boy-Girl-02.psd</u> (or <u>Boy-Girl-02.tif</u>).**

**8. Make sure that the new Figure Layer is selected in the Layers palette of the French House document.**

**9. Resize the elements to fit. Edit, Transform, Scale - type on the bar at the top of the screen: W = 50% and click on the lock symbol next to it to make the height, H the same (50%) (Or hold down the shift key and drag manually by the corner of the box that appears. The shift key maintains the proportions).**

*Figures being scaled smaller*

*Choosing figure placement*

10. **Click inside the rectangle and move the figures to the lower left corner, or wherever you would like, as long as they are close to the bottom of the frame. When you are satisfied with their position, press Enter.**

11. **Save as <u>My French House.psd</u> (or as a TIFF file with the extension .tif but keep the layers).**

12. **KEEP OPEN for the next exercise.**

At this point, the two layers seem to have different lighting situations. The figures are lit with what appears to be sunlight, and the landscape behind is clearly overcast. You can lighten and gray the figures, or you can brighten the background. These options will be explored in the next exercises.

**Elements**® ~ Perform the following instead of the Photoshop® instructions, for the step below. Follow other steps as written.

<u>Step 9</u> - Resize the elements to fit. Image, Transform, Free Transform. Type on the bar at the top of the screen: W = 50%, H = 50%.

130

*( This page left intentionally blank. )*

# 𝒞xercise #18 - Blending Light Sources - *Saturation*

Often, when you wish to combine photographs, you'll find that they may have significantly different color casts and strengths of light and shadow. To make them appear to be illuminated by the same light source, you can change the color saturation of one or both sources.

In this exercise we will work primarily on the figures to blend them more into the light situation of the background.

**1. Open <u>My French House.psd</u> if it is not already open.**

**(If you are skipping ahead, this step may be accessed from the file called <u>My French House.psd</u> in the Next Step Images folder on your CD, Disc Two.)**

**2. Activate the Figure Layer on the Layers palette.**
**3. Image, Adjustments, Levels - Drag center handle so Level Inputs = 0, 1.5, 255, OK.**
**4. Image, Adjustments, Hue/Saturation -  Select Edit = Master; drag the Saturation slider to the left, or type in "-25."**

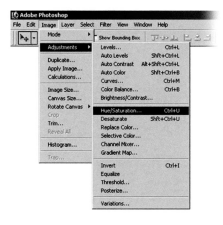 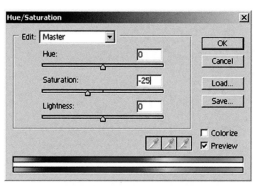

*Set Saturation Slider to -25.*

**5. Click OK.**

My French House.psd
*Before color adjustment.*

French House Overcast.psd
*Figures were grayed down to
match overcast background.*

**6. File, Save As <u>French House Overcast.psd</u>.**
**7. File, Close.**

**Elements**® ~ Perform the following instead of the Photoshop® instructions, for the steps below. Follow other steps as written.

<u>Step 3</u> - Enhance, Adjust Lighting, Levels......same settings as Photoshop®.
<u>Step 4</u> - Enhance, Adjust Color, Adjust Hue/Saturation......same settings as Photoshop®.

# $\mathcal{E}$xercise #19 - Changing Cast Shadows to Create Sunshine Effect
## *Variations, Brightness/Contrast*

The cool overcast light in the previous exercise was relatively easy to achieve. Going to a bright sunny day is not so clear-cut. When the sun is bright, it casts definite shadows by anything it hits. So, the figures in the foreground, if lit by the sun, would have a very specific shadow thrown onto the ground beside them. The house in the background would also cast a shadow. But, before all that, we need to make the houses look as if they are struck by the sun.

This is where one must have a painting background to know intuitively how much contrast and color to add into the background image to approximate a bright sunlight effect. There are no automatic settings in Photoshop® for "changing overcast to sunny". If you have painted outdoors, you know what the natural relationship is between landscape masses in all types of weather conditions. If you have not, then you should study these relationships with a plein-air painter. Photoshop® cannot teach you what to do, it can only respond to what you tell it to do. Photoshop® is not a substitute for painting knowledge.

To approximate the color of sunlight, the colors need to be adjusted toward red and yellow, particularly the light and midtones. Shadows are cooler (bluer) on a sunny day than on an overcast one.

**1. Open <u>My French House.psd</u>.**

> **(If you are skipping ahead, this step may be accessed from the file called <u>My French House.psd</u> in the Next Step Images folder on your CD, Disc Two.)**

**2. Select Background Layer in Layers palette.**

**3. Image, Adjustments, Variations - Click on Original, Set slider one unit to left of center towards Fine, Select Midtones, click 2 times on More Yellow and one time on More Red; Select Shadows, Move slider right towards Coarse by two units, click once on More Blue and Darker, OK. Keep background layer selected.**

**4. Click on Lasso Tool and freehand draw a cast shadow on the ground from the bottom of the stool out to the right of the figures.**

**5. Edit, Copy (Ctrl+C).**

**6. Layer, New, Layer, Enter Name "Shadow Layer" (Or click on "Create a New Layer" icon at the bottom of the Layers palette. Double click on the new layer name "Layer 1" and name Shadow Layer).**

**7. With Shadow Layer now active, Edit, Paste (Ctrl+V) Shadow Layer should appear above the background layer but below the figure layer in the Layers palette. Keep this layer active.**

**8. Image, Adjustments, Brightness/Contrast - set slider to "-40", OK.**

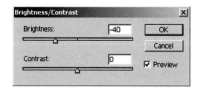

This darkens the "Shadow Layer" to look like a cast shadow under the figures.

**9. Image, Adjustments, Hue/Saturation - set slider on Saturation to "-40", OK.**

French House Sunshine.psd
*Background was brightened to match
the figures and a shadow was added.*

**10. Optional - Shadow Edge Softening:**
        **Click on Erase Tool on Toolbox (Shadow Layer active),**
        **Click on Brushes palette (tab on top right of screen),**
        **Click on Brush Tip Shape in the palette,**
        **Set Diameter to about 60 and Hardness to 0,**
        **Erase around the edges of the distant part of the shadow.**

**11. File, Save As <u>French House Sunshine.psd</u> (or .tif).**
**12. KEEP FILE OPEN for next exercise.**

The cast shadow and warmer colors in the Background layer photo now more nearly match the light intensity and shadow pattern on the figures.

136

**Elements**® ~ Perform the following instead of the Photoshop® instructions, for the steps below. Follow other steps as written.

Step 3 - Enhance, Adjust Color, Color Variations......same settings as Photoshop®.
Step 8 - Enhance, Adjust Lighting, Brightness/Contrast......same settings as Photoshop®.
Step 9 - Enhance, Adjust Color, Adjust Hue/Saturation......same settings as Photoshop®.
Step 10 - There is no "Hardness" control in Elements®, but you can choose a soft edge brush from the drop down menu to achieve this effect, following the instructions for Photoshop®.

# $\mathscr{E}$xercise #20 - Adding Blue Sky - *Layers, Color Range, Move*

You can frequently make a composition more interesting by adding a different sky. The blue between the clouds reinforces the feeling of bright sunlight, so we'll change the plain gray sky to a fluffy-cloud one.

Although the original photo for My French House had no blue sky, we can borrow one from another photo taken on a sunny day.

**1. File, Open <u>Sky.tif</u>. Also open <u>French House Sunshine.psd</u> if it is not already open.**

(**If you are skipping ahead, this step may be accessed from the file called <u>French House Sunshine.psd</u> in the Next Step Images folder on your CD, Disc Two.**)

*Rectangular Marquee Tool*

*Sky.tif*

**2. Click on Rectangular Marquee Tool and drag diagonally from the lower left corner of the sky to the top right corner of the sky to create a selection box around the entire sky.**

If you make a mistake in the selection, you can go to Edit, Undo (Ctrl+Z) or deselect and try making the selection again. To deselect, go to Selection, Deselect (Ctrl+D). The entire sky should now be contained by a crawling rectangular line.

**3. Edit, Copy (Ctrl+C), (Or click on Move Tool and drag to <u>French House Sunshine.psd</u> document window that is open).**

**4. Click on <u>French House Sunshine.psd</u>.**

**5. Edit Paste (Ctrl+V) - creates layer with sky. Rename as "Sky Layer."**

138

(If you are skipping ahead, this step may be accessed from the file called **FrenchHouse-NewSky.psd** in the Next Step Images folder on your CD, Disc Two.)

*New Sky Layer is above the rest of the layers.*

**6. Click on Move Tool (V) and move sky to top of image.**

**7. Edit, Transform, Scale - grab handle at bottom of sky and pull down until it covers all the gray sky in the French House image. Press Enter.**

*Sky layer is stretched further downward.*

**8. Click on Eye of Sky Layer to hide it.**

**9. Activate Background Layer.**

**10. Double click on the Background layer in the Layers palette so that the layer is no longer locked. A New Layer window will appear. Enter the new layer name "House Layer" and press OK. The lock icon will disappear and the new name will appear.**

**11. Select, Color Range, fuzziness=20, Click Eyedropper Tool on sky area of image, Click OK.**

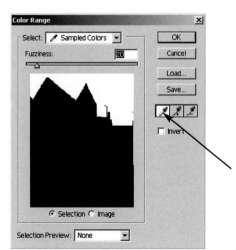

*Click on plain eyedropper and select gray sky area in image by clicking once in gray area.*

**12. Press delete. The white sky is now gone to reveal a transparent area.**

*White sky deleted from*
*Background Layer (House Layer).*

**13. Activate the Sky Layer. Drag the sky layer so that it is below the background layer on the Layers palette. The sky will show through the transparent part of the House Layer.**

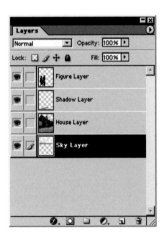

*Sky Layer under House Layer.*
*(Background Layer was renamed to*
*House Layer.)*

French House Sky.psd

**14. File, Save As <u>French House Sky.psd</u>.**

**Elements**® ~ Perform the following instead of the Photoshop® instructions, for the steps below. Follow other steps as written.

<u>Step 7</u> - Edit, Transform, Free Transform....same as Photoshop®.
<u>Step 11</u> - (There is no Select, Color Range tool in Elements®) - Instead, activate the Magic Wand and click in the sky area of the photo, to achieve the same result.

*( This page left intentionally blank. )*

# *Exercise #21* - Casual Photo to Classical Portrait
## *Background Gradient*

This casual photograph was the resource that I used to paint a classical portrait of this mother and daughter. I loved the tender interaction between them in this photo, and since they lived too far away to re-pose them in my studio, I had to work with this image if I wanted to capture that moment. Using all the tools we've worked with prior to this exercise, I extracted them from their background in order to test different colors and styles of background that I might like, before ever putting brush to canvas.

The Gradient Tool has many uses, but this is one of the simplest for setting up a Rembrandt-like lighting situation and background treatment for a portrait.

**Note about "Mother and Child" Next Step Images:** This tutorial will mention several Mother and Child files that are available in the Next Step Images folder, Disc Two. Some of the steps in the Mother and Child exercises require the use of selections. To make it possible for you to use selections that are already done for you, files mentioned during these steps contain pre-made selections. To load a selection in one of these files, go to **Select** (in the top menu), **Load Selection**, then choose from the drop down menu next to **"Channel"**. There are options for Chair Arm, Chair Side Only, and Dress Selection in the Mother and Child Exercises.

**1. Open <u>Mother-Child-01.tif</u>.**

2. Make a copy of the Background layer in the Layers palette.

3. Turn off the original Background layer.

4. Create a new layer and name "White." Drag it below the Background copy layer.

5. Click on the default color button in the Toolbox so that white is the background color indicated in the Toolbox.

6. With the "White" layer activated on the Layers palette go to Edit, Fill, Use Background Color, Press OK (or Ctrl+backspace). (The "White" layer will be filled with white only if the background color on the Toolbox is white). Some of this layer will become visible as you erase from the layer above it in the next step. (This layer is just to help you see what you are erasing. Otherwise, gray and white squares will show up).

7. Select the Background copy layer to make it active in the Layers palette.

8. Remove the background area around the figures using the most convenient tool so that only the figures show on this layer. Now the figures will be surrounded by the white that is visible from the layer beneath it.

*Area around figures is removed.*
*White layer is beneath.*

9. Save as <u>Mother-child-01-bkg.psd</u> (or Mother-child-01-bkg.tif) Keep the layers when saving if you can and KEEP THIS FILE OPEN. (The layers are still being used for this exercise).

10. Create a new layer using the Layers palette, and name it gradient layer.
11. Move the new layer so that it is below the Background copy and above the White layer. Make sure it is activated.

*Layer palette with*
*Gradient layer activated.*

12. Double click on the foreground box part of the foreground/background color icon in the Toolbox to pick a color for the foreground. The color picker menu will appear. Type in new values: R=49, G=14, B=12 to make a dark wine brown. Press OK.

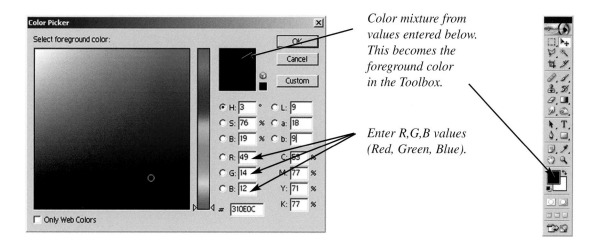

*Color mixture from values entered below. This becomes the foreground color in the Toolbox.*

*Enter R,G,B values (Red, Green, Blue).*

**13. Select the Gradient Tool. A gradient that uses the foreground and background colors should be indicated by the color gradient shown on the top Options bar. Click on this gradient to get the Gradient Editor window. Make sure that the top left corner gradient that is selected is called "Foreground to Background."**

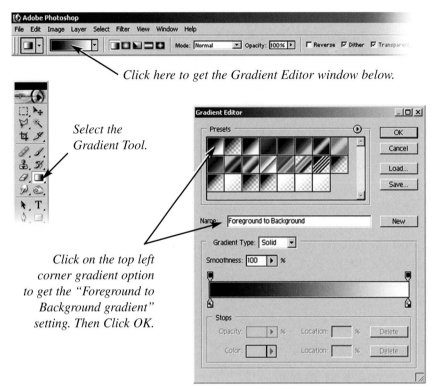

*Click here to get the Gradient Editor window below.*

*Select the Gradient Tool.*

*Click on the top left corner gradient option to get the "Foreground to Background gradient" setting. Then Click OK.*

*Gradient Menu*

**14. While holding down the mouse button, click in the upper left corner about an inch down and in from the corner, then drag outside the upper left corner of the picture. The gradient should fill the area behind the figures, leaving a slightly lighter area near the top left corner. Experiment with different gradient placements to see other effects by changing the starting and ending point. (To undo, go to Edit, Undo or hit Ctrl+Z).**

*Click and drag the Gradient Tool up
and out to the top left corner.*

*The Gradient Layer will fill with the wine
brown color behind the figures.*

**15. File, Save As <u>Mother-child-01-bkg.psd.</u>**

This file is still being used for the exercises so don't close it yet.

**(If you are skipping ahead, this step may be accessed from the file called <u>Mother-child-01-bkg.psd</u> in the Next Step Images folder on your CD, Disc Two.)**

**16. Activate the Background Copy layer.**

**17. Use Magnetic Lasso to select the area that includes the arm of the chair, and all clothes contained between arm and seat of chair.**

After using the Magnetic Lasso - Optional: Change Magnetic Lasso Tool to the Lasso Tool. Hold down the Alt and Shift keys while dragging this tool to add and subtract more areas to and from the selection.

**18. Double click on Foreground Color Selection Box in the Toolbox.**

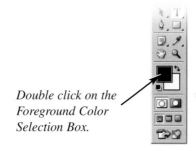

*Double click on the Foreground Color Selection Box.*

**19. Reset color values to R=149, G=10, B=37.**

**20. Change the Gradient Tool to the Paint Bucket Tool and leave it selected.**

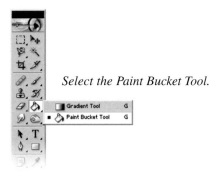

*Select the Paint Bucket Tool.*

**21. Click once on the white arm of the chair (with background copy layer selected).**

This action will fill the white arm of the chair with the bright red color. The area previously selected with the Magnetic Lasso Tool is still selected and active.

Now that you have added color to the arm of the chair, you need to eliminate this area from the larger selection.

**(If you are skipping ahead, this step may be accessed from the file called <u>Mother-child-02-bkg.psd</u> in the Next Step Images folder on your CD, Disc Two.)**

**22. Using the Magic Wand, press Alt-click on the red arm of the chair to deselect it.**

This removes all of the selected red area from the larger selection, which is still active.

23. **Reverse the background/foreground colors in the Toolbox.**
24. **Double click on the (white) Foreground Color Selection Box in Toolbox.**
25. **Reset color values to R=85, G=14, B=45.**
26. **Select the Gradient Tool under the Paint Bucket Tool. Choose the "Foreground to Background" gradient in the gradient menu, accessible at the top of the screen (if it isn't already selected).**
27. **Click on the arm of the chair and drag down to bottom of photo.**

This fills the remainder of the selection with a graded red tone that suggests a solid chair arm with a rolled edge.

**(If you are skipping ahead, this step may be accessed from the file called <u>Mother-child-03-bkg.psd</u> in the Next Step Images folder on your CD, Disc Two.)**

28. **Using the Magic Wand, hold down Shift and click on the red arm of the chair to add it to the current selection.**

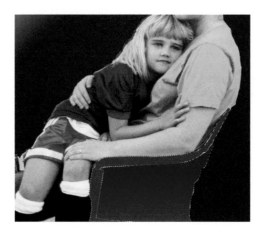

**29. Select Image, Adjustments, Variations. Click on Original first. Choose Darker with Midtones selected, and More Magenta with Shadows selected.**

This makes a darker, richer color in the chair which is more compatible with the very dark background.

**(If you are skipping ahead, this step may be accessed from the file called <u>Mother-child-04-bkg.psd</u> in the Next Step Images folder on your CD, Disc Two.)**

**30. File, Save As <u>Mother-child-01-bkg.psd</u>.**

Keep this file open for the next exercise.

**Elements**® ~ Perform the following instead of the Photoshop® instructions, for the step below. Follow other steps as written.

<u>Step 6</u> - With the "White" layer activated on the Layers palette go to Edit, Fill Layer, Use Background Color.......same as Photoshop®.

152

*( This page left intentionally blank. )*

# *E*xercise #22  - **Replacing Clothes** - *Fill Bucket*

While this is not a refined tool for making changes to clothing, it is useful to test color placement and keep body forms visible for painting. I used this technique to take the eye away from the bright white socks and knees, so the focus of the composition would be on the faces of the two subjects. Because the dress I wanted to paint on the little girl must show the form of the legs under it, I kept the filled area transparent to show some of the light/dark relationships through the skirt.

1. **Using the Magnetic Lasso and the Magic Wand, select all the area that includes the child's shorts, legs, socks, and mother's lap.**

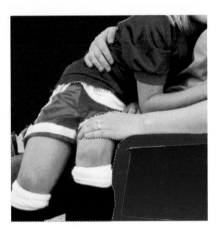

2. **Make new layer. Rename it "Dress."**
3. **Activate Background Copy.**
4. **Use Eyedropper Tool to pick a color from the dark values in the mother's shirt. Click on the desired color.**

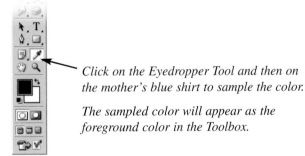

*Click on the Eyedropper Tool and then on the mother's blue shirt to sample the color.*

*The sampled color will appear as the foreground color in the Toolbox.*

5. **Activate Dress layer.**

**6. Use the Paint Bucket under the Gradient Tool to pour the foreground color indicated in the Toolbox into the selection by clicking on it (or use Alt+Backspace to fill the selection with this color).**

**7. Select, Deselect (Ctrl+D).**

**8. File, Save As <u>Mother-child-dress-01.psd</u>.**

**9. Select the arrow next to Opacity at the top of the Layers palette and pull slider to around 80% so that the dress looks about the same as in the following picture.**

This will show the child's legs through the dress layer and give a preview of what the painting color will look like, as well as the color distribution of the masses.

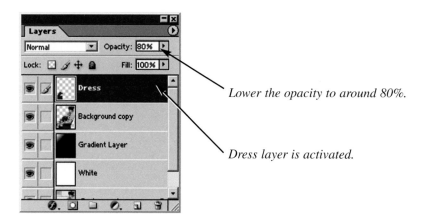

*Lower the opacity to around 80%.*

*Dress layer is activated.*

At this point, you should be seeing the way the painting will fit together.

**10. File, Save As <u>Mother-child-dress-01.psd</u> (or as a .tif file).**

See page 153 for final painting based on this color scheme.

**(This final Mother Child image step may be accessed from the file called <u>MotherChildDress-Done.psd</u> in the Next Step Images folder on your CD, Disc Two.)**

**Elements**® ~ Perform the steps exactly the same as in Photoshop®. The only difference is that the Fill Bucket is found as a separate icon on the Elements® tool bar, and is not a subset of the Gradient tool, as it is in Photoshop®.

*( This page left intentionally blank. )*

# *Ɛ*xercise #23 - **Skintones** - *Posterize, Fade, Desaturate*

Following are the references I used to paint the fleshtones of the two figures. I always have a desaturated grayscale image available for reference to remind me of how few value changes there are within each major facial plane. Review exercises #9, #11, & #12 for in-depth explanation of this process. The posterized fleshtones guide me in the local color of the flesh, but I rely on my experience as a painter from life to estimate the color in the halftone area of the skin (those areas that change temperature within and between value planes.)

**1. Open <u>MotherChild-Closeup.tif</u>.**

**2. Image, Adjustments, Posterize - Levels = 6, Click Preview box on.**
**3. Press OK.**
**4. Edit, Fade Posterize - Use the following recommended values:**
　　　**Opacity = 50%,**
　　　**Mode = Normal,**
　　　**Preview box checked on.**
**5. File, Save As <u>MotherChild-Posterized.tif</u>.**
**6. Image, Adjustments, Desaturate.**
**7. File, Save As <u>MotherChild-BW.tif</u>.**

*Posterized Photo*
*Tone variations are more visible.*

*After Fade Posterize*
*Tone variations are more subtle.*

*After Desaturation*
*Value variations are more visible.*

In the above example, you can see that there are more color variations than value variations in the skin. Once the photo is desaturated after the posterized step, there are fewer sections visible. This demonstrates how the painter must focus greatly on the changes between warm and cool colors more than just the value changes in the skin.

*"Mother's Love" by J. Liliedahl*

This is the final painting called "Mother's Love" by Johnnie Liliedahl. It was painted in oil using all of the related photo references above.

160

**Elements**® ~ Perform the following instead of the Photoshop® instructions, for the steps below. Follow other steps as written.

<u>After Step 1</u>, do the following: Right-click on "Background" layer in Layers Palette, select "Duplicate Layer" and a screen will pop up that says "Background Copy". Press OK. Background Copy layer will be highlighted in dark blue in the Layers palette.
<u>Step 2</u> - Filter, Adjustments, Posterize, Levels = 6.
<u>Step 4</u> - Click on the "Opacity" slider at top of Layers palette and slide to 50%. This takes the place of the "Fade Posterize" function, available only in Photoshop®.

# $\mathscr{E}$xercise #24 - **Removing Facial Blemishes** - *Healing Brush Tool*

You might wonder why this tool is useful for a painter, when you can simply paint out or ignore blemishes. The same could be said for any of the tools we have learned to use in Photoshop®. Blemishes are distractions, and if you can remove them from your resource, your painting job will be easier.

The icon for the Healing Brush Tool is a Band-Aid, and its use is closely related to the Clone Tool in that you must specify an area that has the closest appearance to the blemish you wish to eliminate. In other words, if the area to be cleared is in a light plane, be sure to select a similarly lit plane elsewhere on the face to "heal" from. This tool takes the cloned area and merges it with the blemished area to create a seamless look.

**1. Open <u>Girl with Blemish.tif</u>.**

**2. Click on Healing Brush Tool.**
**3. Look at the Options bar and set Mode = Normal, Source = Sampled**
**4. Click on Brush in the Options bar. Enter:**
                    **Diameter = 10,**
                    **Hardness = 50,**
                    **Spacing = 25.**

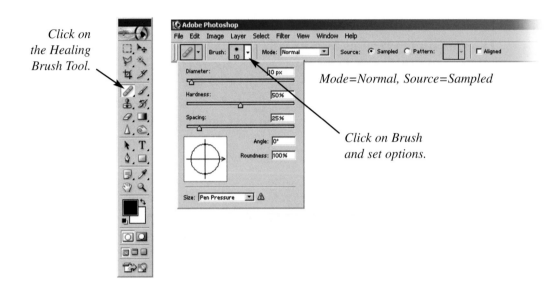

*Click on the Healing Brush Tool.*

*Mode=Normal, Source=Sampled*

*Click on Brush and set options.*

**5. Alt-click in an area on the right cheekbone. This selects the smooth area to be integrated over the blemish.**
**6. Make short clicks to cover only the blemished area.**

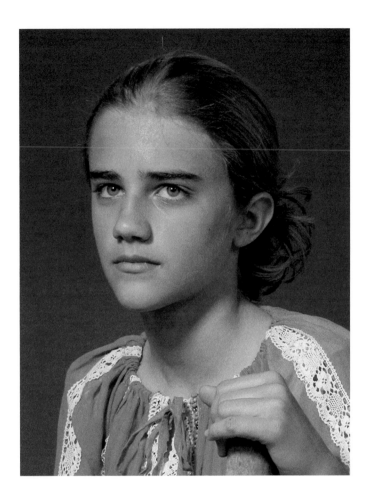

**7. Save As <u>Girl Blemish-free.tif</u>. KEEP OPEN for the next exercise.**

**Elements**® ~ Perform the steps exactly the same as in Photoshop®.

*( This page left intentionally blank. )*

# $\mathscr{E}$xercise #25 - **Synchronize Color Between Photos** - *Color Match*

We have explored a number of ways to match the color of one photo element to fit into a different photo background, mostly because older versions of Photoshop® offered only those methods. Photoshop® CS, however, has made color synchronization more automated with its new Color Match function.

To see how it works, compare the two photographs below, taken on the same day, of the same model, one indoors and one outdoors. These photos show the dramatic difference in the color of light and its influence on fleshtones. The light used to illuminate the indoor model was a 5000-K color-corrected bulb, chosen to emulate natural, outdoor light.

As good as the photograph is, you can still see the overly warm temperature of the fleshtone created by the indoor environment. For many painters, this color cast might be appealing, but if you wanted to use this figure in an outdoor setting, you would have to adjust the color to feel as if the model were actually outdoors.

**1. Open <u>Girl Blemish-free.tif</u> and <u>Girl-Outdoors.tif</u>.**

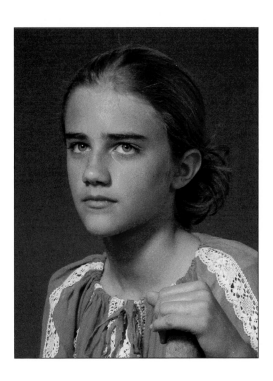 

**2. Click on <u>Girl Blemish-free.tif</u> to be sure it is the active image.**

**3. Click on Image, Adjustments, Match Color, and a new screen will drop down.**

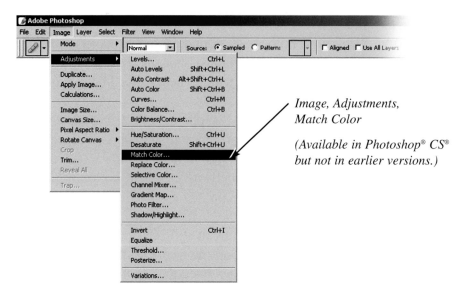

*Image, Adjustments,*
*Match Color*

*(Available in Photoshop® CS®*
*but not in earlier versions.)*

**4. Click Preview ON, look at the bottom of the screen and set Source = <u>Girl-Outdoors.tif</u>.**

The image in the small preview screen will show the image to be matched, while the large image of Girl-Blemish-free automatically changes to the coloration of the source photo.

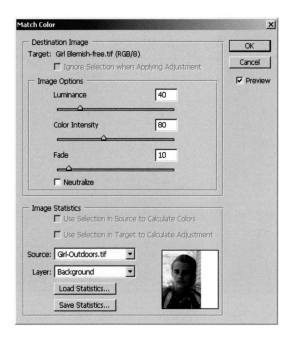

*Match Color Window*

*(Available in*
*Photoshop® CS®*
*but not in earlier*
*versions.)*

5. The default color match isn't always perfect, which is why you have four settings you can change to refine the color. Every situation will require unique settings to match color, but try these settings to fine-tune this pair of photos:

Luminance = 40,
Color Intensity = 80,
Fade = 10,
Neutralize (leave unchecked).

6. Press OK.

*Target Photo*          *Source Photo*          *Color Matched Photo*

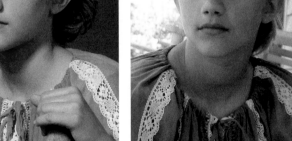

**Elements®** ~ The Color Match feature is available only in Photoshop®.

*( This page left intentionally blank. )*

# $\mathscr{E}$xercise #26 - Color Correcting Photos of Finished Paintings - *Curves*

Perhaps you have taken photographs of paintings (as I have) in the past and you cannot get them to print in the same color range as in the painting. The Curves function in Photoshop® can help correct the problem easily if you have either a pure white, gray or black area in the photograph to use as a reference point. This is sometimes hard to find in a painting, since most artists avoid the use of pure white or black.

If you have already scanned a photograph into the computer and cropped it to size, you may have lost the ability to use this particular feature to color-correct the photograph to match the painting. So, to illustrate how to avoid this particular problem in the future, this exercise will show you not only how to take a photograph properly, but how to correct it easily.

## 1. File, Open <u>Elena-01.tif</u>.

*A white reference in the photo for color correction.*

*Photo of painting before and after color correction using the white reference label. Adjust the photo color before cropping it.*

This is a photograph taken of one of my paintings under mixed lighting. The room included both fluorescent light and incandescent light, so none of the white balance presets on my digital camera would produce accurate results in matching the color of the painting. But if you look closely at the photograph, you will see a "white" piece of paper right above the painting on the easel clamp. Actually, it is a plain white address label that resides permanently on this easel, which I use to photograph my paintings.

As you know, in most endeavors, pre-planning makes all the difference in the outcome of some efforts. Something as simple as a white sticky label will allow you to make all the color corrections necessary to achieve great color output from your computer images and printer.

The secret is to color-correct your image (using this white reference) <u>before</u> you crop your image. If you remove the white reference, then the computer cannot accurately judge the other colors.

**2. Image, Adjustments, Curves.**

The curves window will open showing a diagonal line graph. Ignore this portion of the screen and look for the eyedroppers on the lower right. Hover your mouse over the far right dropper and see that it is the "Set White Point" dropper.

**3. Click on the Set White Point dropper, and move the mouse over to the image. The mouse cursor will change to the eyedropper.**

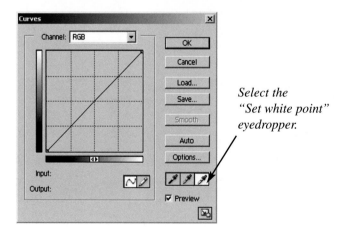

*Select the "Set white point" eyedropper.*

**4. Click on the white reference label inside the photograph.**

(If you cannot see the photograph because it is obscured by the Curves window, drag the window out of the way by clicking and dragging in the blue title bar at the top of the window). The photograph will shift to a near-perfect color range.

**5. Press OK.**

The Curves function is probably the single most powerful function in Photoshop®. You can change color cast, value levels, saturation and intensity.....things you can do with other, single tools. To use it effectively, however, you have to be patient and experimental, and I recommend that you explore its other features on your own, as it is outside the scope of this basic, introductory tutorial.

Curves will change several variables at the same time, and controlling these changes on the graph is tricky. For the novice, it is a confusing, shotgun approach which tends to discourage and frustrate. But, it is useful to those who have thoroughly mastered the other tools explored in the previous Exercises.

**Elements®** ~ The Curves feature is available only in Photoshop®.

*( This page left intentionally blank. )*

# *E*xercise #27 - Composing for Painting

*Extract, Selections, Rotate, Layers, Flip Horizontal,
Polygonal Lasso, Clone, Copy/Paste, Lasso, Levels,
Adjustment Layer, Magnetic Lasso, Variations,
Magic Wand, Brightness/Contrast, Dodge & Burn*

This exercise is a real composition for a painting that I have done. It introduces another feature of Photoshop® that allows you to remove a backdrop easily from the figure so you can impose a figure into a landscape background.

It also confronts a problem of translating the indoor light fall-off on the figure (producing very dark legs) to the larger ambient-light situation of the outdoor landscape. When combining photographs like this, it is useful to critically observe all the light effects on the various elements to make it seem cohesive.

Because I like the strong light pattern on the figure, I will have to change some of the light effects in the landscape elements to conform to the pattern on the girl. But, the legs are much too dark to be believably introduced into the background, so a color and value correction will be necessary for that area. I'll also make some of these corrections to the bucket she holds.

In composing from photographs, sometimes you have to move elements to make them more interesting, or remove them to eliminate distracting elements. We will do both with the components in the background photo.

I often try several different backgrounds for a favorite pose—to see which environment I like best. My first thought was to fill the basket and bucket with seashells and place her in a seascape environment (see preliminary composite below left), but I quickly discarded this idea in favor of the Irish cottage (see finished composite below).

*Vicki on Beach Composite Photo*

*Vicki and Cottage Final Composite Photo*

The final composite was taken from three separate photos, which you will use to complete the exercise.

As I said in the introduction, you must have painting-from-life experience to be able to know what changes to make in projects like this. There is no magic bullet that automatically "fixes" photographs in preparation for painting. Photoshop® is merely a tool—just like a paintbrush. The paintbrush knows nothing by itself. It is totally directed by the artist. So is Photoshop®.

The cottage in the background photo had recently been re-roofed with red tin, and although it adds a nice color note, I preferred the adjacent cottage roof of traditional thatch. We will take the thatch roof and put it onto the white cottage, using all the tools and techniques you have used in previous exercises.

All the changes you are about to make are artistic choices that I made in preparation for using these resources for painting. Many are the same choices I would make if I had the model in Ireland in front of the cottage, and I was painting it entirely on-location. A different artist, in the same place, would make other choices.

**Elements®** ~ The Extract feature is available only in Photoshop®. However, this exercise can be completed in Elements® using methods of erasing the background used in Exercise 16, and combining parts of images from different sources used in Exercise 20. All other functions have been covered in previous exercises.

The Dodge and Burn tools are a subset located under the Sponge tool in the Elements® toolbox, if they are not already visible.

### Step 1 – Copying a Thatched Roof

**1. Open <u>Vicki-Standing.tif</u>, <u>House-ducks photo.tif</u>, and <u>Thatch-source photo.tif</u>.**

Vicki-Standing.tif  House-ducks photo.tif   Thatch-source photo.tif

The first thing to take care of is replacing the tin roof with a thatched one. The only problem is that the roofs are receding away from the viewer in different directions, so we need to have the houses face the same direction.

**2. Click on <u>Thatch-source photo.tif</u>.**

**3. Image, Rotate Canvas, Flip Canvas Horizontal.**

**4. Activate Polygonal Lasso Tool.**

**5. Click and select a portion of the bottom edge of the roof.**

**6. Edit, Copy (or drag selected area with the Move Tool to the House photo with ducks).**

**7. Click on <u>House-ducks photo.tif</u>.**

**8. Edit, Paste.**

The thatched roof will appear on a new layer in the middle of the image.

**9. Activate the Move Tool.**

**10. With Layer 1 (the roof layer) selected in the Layers palette, move the thatch roof and align in the upper right corner.**

<u>House-Ducks-02.psd</u>
*(New thatch roof added.)*

**11 . Edit, Free Transform - Grab corner handles and position thatch in place of the tin roof. Press enter when finished changing the size and rotation.**

**12. If you are missing a small piece on the right side, use the Clone Tool to fill in.**

**13. File, Save As <u>House-Ducks-02.psd.</u> KEEP ALL FILES OPEN for the next exercise.**

## Step 2 – Copying Grass and Ducks

Next, you will copy the grass from the thatched cottage photo to put into the target House-duck photo.

BEFORE: <u>House-Ducks-02.psd</u>
*With new thatch roof.*

AFTER: <u>House-Ducks-02.psd</u>
*Grass pasted on layer
over duck layer*

1. Click on <u>Thatch-source photo.tif</u>.
2. Select the Polygonal Lasso Tool.
3. Set the Feather = 20px in the Options bar.
4. Use the Polygonal Lasso Tool to select the lower left corner including the gravel path.
5. Drag selected area with the Move Tool to the <u>House-Ducks-02.psd</u> window. A new layer will be created with the patch of grass on it that was selected.

Optional - Instead of dragging a layer you can also use Copy and Paste. On the layer with the selection Edit, Copy (Ctrl+C). Click on <u>House-Ducks-02.psd</u>, Edit, Paste. The selected grass will appear on a new layer.

6. Double-click on the new layer name and rename "Grass."
7. Use Ctrl+T to select the Free Transform Tool. Drag the new patch of grass so that the walking path lines up with the foundation of the house and covers the old path. Cover the ducks in the foreground. Press Enter when finished changing the size and rotation.
8. Select the Eraser Tool, Enter options on the top Options bar, Brush = 59 ragged shape (from the drop down menu), Mode = Brush, Opacity 80%. Erase around the edges of the grass layer to integrate it into the background grass layer below. Erase grass that covers haystack in background. (If this brush is slow, do only a little at a time).

9. **Click on Eye icon on Grass layer to turn it off.**
10. **Click on New Layer icon and label "Move Ducks."**
11. **Drag the "Move Ducks" layer to the top layer of the Layers palette.**
12. **Click on Background layer.**
13. **Lasso Duck group in center of photo.**
14. **Edit, Copy (Ctrl+C).**
15. **Click on "Move Ducks" layer, Edit, Paste (Ctrl+V)—The ducks now appear on their own layer.**
16. **Select, Deselect (Ctrl+D).**

BEFORE: House-Ducks-02.psd
*Grass is pasted on new layer above
the original Background layer*

AFTER: House-Ducks-02.psd
*Ducks are copied and pasted onto
a new layer above the grass layer.*

17. **Click on Eye icon on the Grass layer to turn on.**
18. **Click on "Move Ducks" layer.**
19. **Select Move (V) Tool, grab ducks and move to left at same horizontal level as before, to the left of a plumb line dropped from the red door.**
20. **Edit, Transform, Flip Horizontal (ducks will flip to face the left now).**

**21. Zoom in and carefully erase around the ducks, Select Eraser Tool and enter values at top. Brush=21 (choose from drop down menu), Mode = Brush, Opacity=100, Flow=100. Click on the Airbrush button (with an airbrush icon on it) to the right so that it is selected.**

*The "Move Ducks" layer is moved and flipped horizontally.*

*Extra grass is erased from around the ducks on the "Move Ducks" Layer.*

**22. Save as <u>House-Ducks-02.psd</u>.**

FINAL: <u>House-ducks-02.psd</u>
*The composition was rearranged using copies of grass and ducks.*

**23. File, Close.**

## Step 3 – Extracting a Figure

Next, you will remove the background around the girl by using the Extract Tool. Before you can place the figure into the background, however, we have to change the value and temperature of the legs and feet, which are too dark and gray to suggest a natural light situation.

BEFORE: Vicki-Standing.tif     AFTER: Vicki-Extracted.psd

Let's correct the feet and legs first.

1. **Click on the file called <u>Vicki-Standing.tif</u> or open it if it isn't already open.**
2. **To duplicate the Background layer, Right-click on Background Layer, Duplicate Layer, OK (or drag layer over the duplicate layer icon instead).**
3. **Image, Adjust, Levels, Input levels = 0, 2.7, 255, OK.**
4. **Choose the Magnetic Lasso Tool. Outline both feet and legs.**
   (Settings in the Options bar can remain the same as last time: Feather=0, check Anti-aliased box, Width=10 px, Edge Contrast=10%, Frequency=57).
5. **Select, Save Selection. Under "Name" in the Window that appears enter: Feet and Legs, Click OK.**

6. Drag Background Copy to trash can; selection now shows on Background layer.

7. Right-click on Background Layer, Duplicate Layer, OK.

8. Image, Adjust, Variations.

9. Click on Original, be sure slider is halfway between Fine and Coarse, uncheck clipping.

10. Choose Shadows, click twice on Lighter, click twice on More Red, click once on More Yellow.

11. Choose Midtones, click Lighter.

12. Choose Highlights, click twice on More Blue, OK.

13. Edit, Copy (Ctrl+C).

14. Click on New Layer Icon, Name it Feet and Legs, OK. This layer should be the top layer in the Layers palette.

15. Edit Paste (Ctrl+V) - to put new legs on the Feet and Legs layer.

Vicki-Standing.tif

Vicki-Standing.psd
*After color adjustment
of Legs and Feet*

16. File, Save As <u>Vicki-Standing.psd</u>.

17. Click Eye icon for Feet and Legs layer to turn off.

18. **Turn Eye icon off for Background layer.**
19. **Select Background Copy layer.**
20. **Go to Filter or Image (Where to go depends on what version of program you have. 6.0–Image and 7.0–Filter), Extract - large menu with window shows up. Choose Brush size 50, Highlight = Green, Fill = Red.**
21. **Choose the Edge Highlighter Tool at top of menu on left bar. Place half on figure and half on background and outline hair only. Change Brush size to 20 and outline entire exterior figure. For holes inside elbow, etc., click on Smart Highlighting box and place crosshair circle half on figure and background to complete tiny outlining.**
22. **Select Bucket Tool and fill inside the figure with red. Check for leaks. If outline is not firmly connected all the way around the form, the red will leak out into areas of background. To backtrack, choose the Eraser Tool and click inside the figure to undo the bucket. Connect broken outline, and refill figure with Bucket Tool. OK.**

*Extract Filter Menu*
*Outline using the Edge Highlighter.*

*Select the Bucket Tool and*
*click within the outlined figure.*

23. **If some parts of blouse, bucket or dress are transparent on the edges, you can use the History Brush to replace them.**

24. **Click on the Feet and Legs Layer eye icon to bring them back.**
25. **Lasso any parts of the rug to remove on the Background copy layer with the Delete key.**
26. **Layer, Merge Visible, The Feet and Legs layer will merge onto the Background Copy layer.**
27. **Save As <u>Vicki-Extracted.psd</u>.**
28. **File, Close.**

<u>Vicki-Extracted.psd</u>

29. **Drag the hidden Background Layer to the Trash, Save.**

## Step 4 – Adjusting the Lighting of the Landscape

Before we assemble the figure into the background photo, we need to make their lighting more similar. I want to have the effect of a sunlit day. The landscape will have to be adjusted so its lighting is closer to that of the figure.

BEFORE: House-ducks-02.psd

AFTER: HouseDucks-NewColor.tif
*Color adjusted to the lighting of a sunny day.*

1. **File, Open House-Ducks-02.psd.**
2. **Layer, Flatten Image.**
3. **Image, Adjustments, Variations- Click on Original, Select Midtones, Set Fine/Course slider to the middle, Click on More Yellow once.**
4. **Choose the Magic Wand Tool. Set Tolerance at the top to 50.**
5. **Click on white walls. Hold down the Shift key while clicking and adding to the selection so that almost all of the white wall is selected.**
6. **Image, Adjustments, Brighten/Contrast, Contrast=50.**
7. **Image, Adjustments, Variations- Click on Original, Set Fine/Course slider to the middle, Highlights, Click on More Yellow five times, Click on More Red five times, Click OK.**
8. **Select, Deselect (Ctrl+D).**
9. **File, Save As HouseDucks-NewColor.tif.**

## Step 5 – Combining Two Photos

1. **File, Open <u>HouseDucks-NewColor.tif</u>.**
2. **File, Open <u>Vicki-Extracted.psd</u>.**
3. **Activate Background Copy Layer on the Vicki-Extracted file.**
4. **Select All (Ctrl+A) (or just choose the Move Tool and drag to the <u>HouseDucks-NewColor.tif</u> window).**
5. **Edit, Copy (Ctrl+C).**
6. **Click on the <u>HouseDucks-NewColor.tif</u> window. Edit, Paste (Ctrl+V).**

   The girl appears in the landscape photo.

7. **Close <u>Vicki-Extracted.psd</u>.**
8. **Rename the Layer 1 layer with the large picture of Vicki as "Vicki."**

*Vicki was added to the sunny background.*

As she is now, she seems too large in proportion to the house.

9. **Edit, Transform, Scale, Hold down the Shift key (to keep proportions from being altered) and drag corner handle of girl's image until it is smaller, as in the final composition. Release the mouse button and then the shift key. Press Enter when finished resizing.**
10. **Place Vicki in the composition as shown in the final example.**

*Vicki was sized smaller and moved.*

**11. File, Save As <u>VickiandHouse.psd</u> and KEEP FILE OPEN.**

186

## Step 6 – Enhancing a Shadow with the Burn and Dodge Tools

The terms Burn and Dodge are photographic development lab terms. In traditional photography a photo negative is exposed to photosensitive paper in a darkroom using light. The paper starts out white but is darkened in the areas that receive light through the negative. The <u>Burn</u> Tool is used to allow more light to go to a specific area on photo paper so that area is exposed and <u>darkened</u> more. The <u>Dodge</u> Tool blocks the light in whatever area it is used so that the photo paper will be less exposed and <u>lighter</u> in that area. The resulting photo will then be darkened (Burn) and lightened (Dodge) in certain areas that weren't on the original negative.

First we will make a shadow under Vicki to suggest a sunny day. To make the shadow look more like a real shadow, we will darken it where it is closest to Vicki using the Burn Tool. The far edges of the shadow will be faded away in a gradual and natural way using the Dodge Tool.

1. **Open <u>VickiandHouse.psd</u> if it is not already open.**
2. **Create a new blank layer and drag it between the Vicki layer and Background layer. Double click on the name "Layer 1" and call it "Shadow."**
3. **Select the Lasso Tool, Feather=15 at the top, Draw the outline of a shadow under Vicki.**
4. **Activate the Background Layer, Edit, Copy (or Ctrl+C).**
5. **Activate the Shadow Layer, Edit, Paste (or Ctrl+V).**
6. **Image, Adjustments, Brightness/Contrast, Brightness = -60, Press OK.**
7. **Select the Burn Tool, Set Values at the top menu: Range = Midtones, Values = 80%. Darken the shadow area under and near the feet.**
8. **Select the Dodge Tool (under the Burn Tool), set values at top: Range = Midtones, Values = 50%. Erase slightly around the far edges of shadow so that it looks like the final picture.**

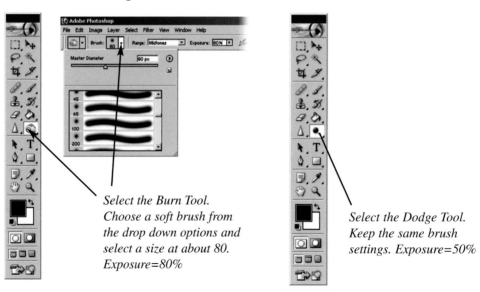

*Select the Burn Tool. Choose a soft brush from the drop down options and select a size at about 80. Exposure=80%*

*Select the Dodge Tool. Keep the same brush settings. Exposure=50%*

*Shadow after Brightness = -60*
*(Grass was darkened.)*

*Shadow was darkened on left*
*around feet with Burn Tool.*

*Shadow was lightened on right side*
*with Dodge Tool.*

*Finished Composition,* VickiandHouse-Done.psd

*"Country Girl"*
*Original Oil Painting by Johnnie Liliedahl*

The artist created this painting using the composite photographs
shown in Exercise 27 as references.

# WORKING WITH YOUR OWN PHOTOS

### Image Resolution

The resolution of an image is described in units of ppi, or pixels per inch. All of the photos provided with this tutorial are already at the recommended resolution of 300ppi. An image that is too low in resolution will appear pixelated or blurred when printed even though it may look fine on screen. When scanning photos, the most important feature to manually enter is the resolution.

*Photo of Sangemini, 300ppi*    *Photo of Sangemini, 60ppi*

It is important to know what resolution you need for your image before working with an image-editing program. For something that is going to be printed, a resolution of 300ppi, or higher, is recommended. If you are only going to be looking at the image on screen, a resolution of only 72ppi is needed. Of course, a higher resolution file takes more storage space on your computer, but storing files at a higher resolution is preferable if the images are ever to be printed. Once you have decreased the resolution of an image, <u>and saved the file</u>, you have thrown away some of the visual information data that goes with that file, and it can never be retrieved.

Photos at 300ppi are considered to be safe for printing but there are exceptions to the rule with other types of images. Some images may print well for painting references at a lower resolution than 300ppi such as the example of Becky on page 101 at 72ppi resolution.

## Changing Image Size and Resolution

When increasing the dimensions (or resolution) of a photo in Photoshop®, the relationship of the original resolution to the size of the photo must be considered. If one of these aspects is increased, the other must decrease. You can't increase one aspect without sacrificing (and decreasing) the other. Photoshop® can show this relationship while these values are entered.

Important Note: One can use the Photoshop® settings to increase the size and resolution of a photo without lowering either the size or resolution, but this will create a photo with an inaccurate resolution. The file will take more memory to store but it won't have improved visual detail. It is wasting kilobytes or megabytes on your hard drive and this should be avoided.

## Increasing the Resolution for Printing

When you open your digital camera photos in Photoshop® for the first time, they may have low resolution of only 72ppi and be too physically large (i.e. 22 x 28). You may want to make the resolution 300ppi for future printing purposes.

To increase the resolution and have the dimensions lower accordingly, go to Image and then Image Size. Uncheck the Resample Image box first. (The Constrain Proportions box will stay checked.) Then enter 300ppi under resolution. As you enter the higher resolution value, the dimensions will decrease proportionately. Click OK.

*Uncheck the Resample Image box first. Then enter values next to Resolution.*

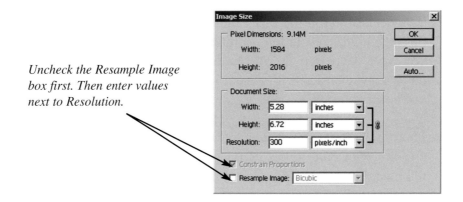

### Decreasing the Dimensions and Keeping the Resolution

Now your photo may have the correct resolution of 300ppi for printing but perhaps the dimensions are still too large. To decrease the dimensions of a file in Photoshop® and keep the resolution the same, go to Image in the top Menu, and choose Image Size. In the new window, <u>check both the Constrain Proportions and Resample Image</u> boxes at the bottom. Second, enter the number of inches or other units under Document Size. The resolution value will remain the same but the dimensions will decrease. Then choose OK.

When the Resample box is checked, the dimensions and size are locked except for the values that are entered manually.

### Enlarging Photos

This is somewhat of an exception to the rules above. Perhaps you would like to make a large poster-sized, unpixelated photo that will be 300ppi out of something a small image. There is a way to do this without degrading the image quality too greatly.

Go to Image, Image Size and check the Resampling box. Bicubic resampling should be indicated next to it and the Constrain proportions box is checked. Now change the values at the top from pixels to percent and enter 110 next to the width and height. Both will say 110 percent. Press OK.

Repeat this same action of enlarging by 10% until you get the desired dimensions. The program will automatically fill in some of the missing detail to create a larger image with very little loss of detail. Using larger percentages than 110% at one time will create a greater loss of image quality.

### Camera Raw Images

Most consumer cameras, at the writing of this book, do not have the option of choosing the Camera Raw Image resolution, so working with Raw files has not been addressed in this edition of the tutorial. If you have a higher-end digital camera that does give this option, then you will want to use that format for your painting reference photos.

Each camera has its own proprietary format for Raw images and generally requires that you use the camera brand's software to open the Raw file so it can be changed to a readable format by photo-imaging programs, such as .tif, .jpg, etc. Also, these software programs will have their own editing functions that will allow you to do many of the functions you have learned in Photoshop®.

Obviously, it would be better to work on the Raw image in its original proprietary state before changing it to another format. But the printing, skewing, cropping and resizing options offered by Photoshop® will still be useful, even if you do all your color corrections in the other software.

# AFTERWORD

It goes without saying that I have hardly scratched the surface of what the Photoshop® program can do for you. But I have deliberately chosen to stop at this point so that this does not become one of those books that is so large that it intimidates the beginning user by its very size.

I own many such books on Photoshop®, and have learned a great deal from them, but it is sometimes very difficult to find the small detail that is useful for a painter to know.

My own discovery of Photoshop's® potential continues, and there will perhaps be an updated edition of this book in the future. One particular feature that I have left unexplained is the Curves function. I believe that a thorough understanding of the basic functions outlined in this book is a prerequisite to understanding how Curves works, and how you can release its potential.

Your comments and suggestions are welcome, and you may offer them by e-mail to me at johnnie@lilipubs.com.

Any errors or omissions are my own, and I hope that this introduction to Photoshop® will enhance and enrich your paintings, as I believe it has for mine.

Happy Painting!

*Liliedahl*

# LILIEDAHL

## ILLUMINATIONS VIDEO SERIES

## A Full Course in Painting for Both
## the Beginner and More Experienced Painter

This comprehensive series provides the skills
and knowledge that lay the foundation for better painting.

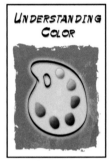

**DI-1**    **$55**

**DI-2**    **$55**

**DI-3**    **$55**

**DI-4**    **$55**

**DI-5**    **$55**

*All on DVD!*

*If you are unsure of your skills as a painter, and need to know more basic painting terminology, theory, and techniques, you would enjoy viewing and collecting these videos. They were filmed to capture the fundamental information presented in the School of Oil Painting curriculum here in our studio. Used together, the painting skills and computer skills will enable you to create more beautiful paintings from your original photographic resources.*
*– Johnnie Liliedahl*

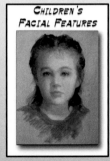

**DI-6**    **$55**

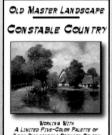

**DI-7**    **$55**

**DI-8**    **$55**

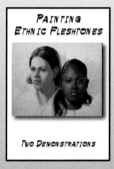

**DI-9**    **$55**

**DI-10**    **$55**

**LVP**

To order these and other videos, Call/Fax TOLL-FREE **877-867-0324 or 281-867-0324**, or visit our website at: **www.lilipubs.com**

Liliedahl Video Productions, 808 South Broadway Street, La Porte, Texas 77571-5324.   Add $8.50 s&h (per order) for UPS delivery; TX residents add 7.75% tax

# LILIEDAHL SCHOOL OF CLASSICAL OIL PAINTING

## *Looking for Good Basic Instruction in Painting Theory and Techniques?*

*Join the ever-growing number of painters who take advantage of the accelerated courses offered in our studio workshops (Houston, TX). These courses are designed for the busy adult who hasn't the time for a four-year period of study. With total immersion, disciplined practice and a sound curriculum presented in each workshop, you will be amazed at how quickly you can overcome your lack of formal training in a traditional art atelier. Our core program is based on six workshops, each featured below. For this year's schedule and in-depth descriptions of each workshop and its contents, visit our website and click through to the School of Classical Oil Painting.*

*– Johnnie Liliedahl*

### COLOR COMPOSITION & DESIGN
Color, as it relates to Still Life, Landscape and Portrait

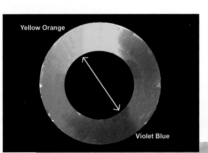

### OLD MASTER FLEMISH METHOD
Bistre/Ebauche

### STILL LIFE
The foundation class for learning to draw and paint the Fine Art way

### LANDSCAPES
Learn how to paint landscapes from life– all in the studio

### OLD MASTER VENETIAN METHOD
Grisaille

### PORTRAITS
Learn to draw and paint the live model